The Safe Child Book

The Safe Child Book

By
Sherryll Kerns Kraizer

Illustrated by
Mary Kornblum

A DELL TRADE PAPERBACK

A DELL TRADE PAPERBACK

Published by
Dell Publishing Co., Inc.
1 Dag Hammarskjold Plaza
New York, New York 10017

Produced by James Charlton Associates

Library of Congress Cataloging in Publication Data

Kraizer, Sherryll Kerns.
  The safe child book.

  Bibliography: p.
  1. Child molesting—Prevention—Study and teaching—United States. 2. Abduction—Prevention—Study and teaching—United States. 3. Child abuse—Prevention—Study and teaching—United States. 4. Day-care centers—United States—Evaluation. I. Title.
HQ72.U53K73 1985b   362.7′044
ISBN 0-385-29403-4
ISBN 0-440-57596-6 (pbk.)
Library of Congress Catalog Card Number: 84-25995

A hardcover edition of this work is available from Delacorte Press, 1 Dag Hammarskjold Plaza, New York, New York 10017.

For my parents

Acknowledgments

I want to thank first and foremost my husband, Al Kraizer, for his unwavering support and encouragement of this work. He has been a friend, a critic and a partner, always contributing energy, insight, and love.

Barbara Binswanger, who not only saw the potential of this book but made it possible by her support and perseverance.

Jim Charlton, my book packager, for his enthusiasm, understanding and professionalism. Without him, I would still be trying to write this book.

Betsy Ryan, for her invaluable assistance in cleaning up the first draft and her partnership in completing the final manuscript.

Susan Moldow, my editor at Dell, for taking this work as seriously as I do.

I am grateful for the advice and feedback of my manuscript readers: Suzanne Barchers, Cynthia Graves, Phyllis Graves, Paula Kascel, Nancy Graves Kravitz, Marilyn Miller, Perry-Lynn Moffitt, Carol Traut and Dave Wahl.

Finally, special thanks are due all the women who have contributed their time, energy and enthusiasm to the development of the Children Need To Know program from which this book evolved: Suzanne Adams, Margie Antal-Green, Margaret Casart, Gina Deal, Marilou Edwards, Gage Evans-Norris, Karen Farrar, Sandy Griffin, Mandy Keiley, Kathy Hardison, Teresa Howes, Kathy Langston, Helen Mann, Ellen Masko, Jean Martini, Kathy Marvin, Jean Mensendick, Marilyn Miller, Valerie Norris, Betty O'Neill, Judy O'Shea, Adrian Rainey, Connie Smith, and Theresa Vigil.

Contents

1 THE BASICS 11

The Problem, Safety Without Fear, Children Need to Know,
The Safest Child of All, Prevention Begins Early, How to Use
This Book

2 THE WHAT IF GAME 21

A Window into Your Children's Minds, Getting Started, The
What If Game Should Never Frighten, Special Issues for
Children of Different Ages, What Ifs—How Parents Play, One
Essential What If Question, When Children Ask Questions
Repeatedly, What If Checklist

3 UNDERSTANDING SEXUAL ABUSE 35

What Is Sexual Abuse?, Why Sexual Abuse Is So Destructive,
Who Are the Perpetrators?, Incest, Stepparents as Abusers,
Do Children Abuse One Another?, The Tools of the Child
Abuser, Why Children Let It Continue, Do Children Lie About
Sexual Abuse?, Sexual Abuse and Sex Education, Playing
Doctor

4 PREVENTING SEXUAL ABUSE 45

Your Body Belongs to You, How to Say No, Private Parts,
Double Messages, How Should Adults Respond?, Letting
Children Decide, Examples for Three- to Six-year-olds,
Examples for Seven- to Twelve-year-olds, I'm Going to Tell,
Tattling, Preventing Emotional Coercion, No More Secrets,
Children and Secrecy, Adults Have Rules Too, Whom Do You
Tell, Who Else Can You Tell?

5 IDENTIFYING STRANGERS 59

Who Are Stranger Offenders?, Strangers—The Child's Point Of View, What Bad Guys Look Like, How Do You Tell?, So Now What Do You Do?, Preparing to Change the Rules, Strangers—The Parents' Point of View, Personal Safety for Children, Expanding Privileges, Establishing a Common Ground

6 PREVENTING ABUSE AND ABDUCTION BY STRANGERS 69

Rule 1—The Arm's Reach Plus, Rule 2—Don't Talk to Strangers, But They Knew My Name, Rule 3—Don't Take Things From Strangers, Not Even Your Own Things, Rule 4— Don't Go Anywhere with a Stranger, The Code Word, Feeling Funny Inside, Relaxing the Rules, What If They Get Me Anyway?, Children Prevent Abuse and Abduction, Stranger Rules Checklist

7 STAYING ALONE 85

Ground Rules, Staying Alone Checklist, Negotiating Ground Rules, Answering the Telephone, Safe Telephone Procedures for General Calls, Special Types of Calls, Answering the Door, Safe Door Procedures, Being Scared: Fear Versus Being Spooked, Knowing Normal Noises, Emergencies, Resources for Help, Staying Alone Safely

8 MAKING EXCEPTIONS TO THE RULES 95

Being Polite, Lying and Breaking Promises, Blind Obedience

9 CHOOSING CHILD CARE 101

Licensed and Unlicensed Group Day Care, Checklist for Licensed and Unlicensed Group Care, Taking Your Own Concerns Seriously, Supervised and Unsupervised Family Day Care, Checklist for Supervised and Unsupervised Family Day Care, In-home and Out-of-home Individual Care, Baby-sitters

10   WHEN CHILDREN ARE SEXUALLY ABUSED   111

How Children Tell Us, How Should We Respond?, What
About Reporting?, What Happens Next?, Is Therapy
Necessary?

11   BEING A RESPONSIBLE ADULT   119

Rules for Responsible Strangers, Lost Children, Children We
Know, Child Advocacy

APPENDIX   123

For More Information, Acknowledgments, Annotated
Bibliography, References

CHAPTER 1

The Basics ...

THE PROBLEM

We don't like to accept the fact that our children are in danger of being kidnapped or subjected to sexual abuse. We don't really know how to think about it, or what to do to adequately protect our families. Some of us dismiss the possibility, thinking "I'm pretty safety conscious" or "I watch out for my children, it could never happen to them" or "My parents never had to worry about this. Has so much changed?"

The distressing fact is our children are very vulnerable. Consider these statistics:

▶ According to the National Center for Missing and Exploited Children, up to 50,000 children disappear each year, and those cases remain unsolved.

▶ The 1953 Kinsey report found that one in every four women in the study had been sexually abused as a child.

▶ In 1981 researcher Diana Russell reported that 38 percent of the women participating in her study had experienced sexual abuse by age eighteen.

▶ The Child Sexual Abuse Prevention Project reported that 30 to 46 percent of all children are sexually assaulted in some way by age eighteen.

▶ Cases involving boys are less often reported, but recent research indicates they may be at equal risk as girls.

▶ Experts agree that 85 to 90 percent of all incidents of sexual abuse take place with someone the child knows and trusts, not a stranger.

▶ David Finkelhor, a leading researcher in the field, reported in 1979 that 26 percent of the students in his survey were sexually abused by a member of their family.

▶ The Children's Defense Fund estimates that 5.2 million children thirteen and under are left without adult supervision each day.

These facts are startling and hard to believe, and people often feel the statistics must be exaggerated. But most adults who were abused as children don't talk about it. I remember one small PTA meeting I was asked to attend to discuss prevention of sexual abuse and abduction. After I reported the magnitude of the problem, one woman said to me, "That just isn't possible, I don't know anyone who was sexually abused as a child." Very quietly the woman across from her said, "I was" and a moment later the man beside me followed with "I was too."

The problem, whether it is escalating or simply being more openly discussed, is very real, and the fact that our children are so vulnerable can be overwhelming. There are many avenues that we as a society can take that could lead to change: tougher legislation is one; more vigorous prosecution, and stiffer penalties for perpetrators are another; better educational programs in schools is a third. This book however, is about what *you and your family* can do to prevent sexual abuse and abduction.

SAFETY WITHOUT FEAR

Keeping your children safe means looking at what you say and do with them from a new perspective. It means changing the way you think about their safety and creating some new rules for your children and for yourself.

The purpose of this book is to:

▶ **give you a basic understanding of sexual abuse and abduction**

▶ **provide specific personal safety training skills, techniques, and examples to use with your children**

▶ **encourage you to portray the world to your children as a basically positive place**

▶ **lessen your anxiety about your children's safety so you can allow them the freedom of movement they need as they grow up**

As you read this book, it is useful to notice what portions are particularly upsetting to you, those that make you want to stop reading, or that seem hard to understand. These can be clues to your own emotions and personal experiences. As you teach prevention to your children, your feelings as well as your ideas will affect what you say and do. The more you understand about your own feelings, the more effective you can be with your children.

One of the first things to remember is that scare tactics don't work. They tend to overwhelm and paralyze children instead of protecting them. For example, warning children "Don't take candy from strangers because it might be poisoned" conjures up a very negative image about the world in which they live but doesn't give a useful guideline. It is also ineffective. Children don't really understand what the phrase as a whole means. As a result, they either take things from people who seem nice because they don't realize these people are strangers, or they overreact and won't take anything from anyone.

You've taught or will teach your children how to swim and how to cross the street without resorting to fear tactics. You didn't tell them horror stories about children who have been killed by careless drivers in order to ensure their safety on the streets. Instead, you've probably dealt with these potentially dangerous situations by giving your children basic rules to follow. We're going to take that same sensible approach in this book to teach prevention of sexual abuse and abduction.

The Safe Child Book will show you how to teach prevention of sexual abuse and abduction without fostering the idea that the world is an evil place in which the people your children love and trust the most might hurt them. It is possible to teach children safety rules using positive, reassuring techniques. We can address the risks effectively and still allow our children to feel loved and nurtured as they grow up in a less than perfect world.

Ultimately, sexual abuse and abduction prevention must be taught directly to your children. Why? Because even those parents who "never" leave their children alone might not be around when a situation arises. You can't be on guard every minute: You might be in the backyard while your child is playing on the front lawn; or you could be in aisle three buying apples while your child is in aisle four looking at the cereal boxes. In reality, it's impossible for you to be available *all the time* to avert a threat to your child.

CHILDREN NEED TO KNOW

The Safe Child Book is based on the Children Need to Know prevention of sexual abuse and personal safety training program, which I developed in 1981 in response to the work I had done with children who had experienced abuse. The program focuses on prevention of sexual abuse and abduction, as well as safety for children who stay home alone. To date, it has been presented to over 50,000 children and their parents.

The evidence that the program works comes from the parents who have called me to say their children successfully stopped an attempted sexual abuse after participating in the program. The most striking endorsement, however, comes from the families whose children have averted abduction by using the techniques they had learned. In each case, the parents were visibly shaken and their children were calmly saying things like "I don't know why you are so upset. You taught me what to do and I did it. Everything is okay now."

Developing your children's ability to take care of themselves as a natural part of what they do every day is the intention of this book.

THE SAFEST CHILD OF ALL

This personal safety training program is built around some simple ideas about the abilities of children:

Children can and must be responsible for their own well-being at times. They are often their own best resource, and training sharpens their ability to be more responsible for themselves when they need to be.

There is really only one person who is with your child all the time and who can keep him or her out of danger—that is, himself or herself. At the moment of risk, the only things our children can fall back on are their own instincts and the training we've given them. That has to be enough.

Children can and should speak up for themselves. They definitely have something to say about what happens to them. What they need is permission to say it and the training to say it effectively and appropriately.

Children as young as three, four, and five are able to generalize, to take the rules and guidelines we give them for one situation and apply them to another.

Tickling is a good example. If too much tickling makes your children feel uncomfortable or "funny" inside and they have your permission to say stop, they can generalize and transfer that permission to another situation in which they are being touched in a way they don't like and again say stop.

Children are capable of making judgments—that is, they can consider the alternatives and make decisions for themselves.

A good example is the five-year-old who told me about a time she refused to take something out of the oven when the baby-sitter asked her to. She knew that the dish might be too heavy and she'd drop it or too hot and she'd burn herself. She was right.

Another preschooler told me about a time his uncle asked to sleep in his bed with him. He said, "No, my bed's for me, not for big people." No one had ever discussed this possibility with him, he just knew what made sense to him and said no.

> **The best overall defense your children have against sexual abuse and abduction is:**
> ► **a sense of their own power**
> ► **the ability to accurately assess and handle a wide variety of situations**
> ► **knowing where and how to get help**
> ► **knowing they will be believed**
>
> **Children have a right to be safe without being afraid. Children who have been taught to think for themselves are the safest children of all**

PREVENTION BEGINS EARLY

Prevention training can be a natural part of growing up, particularly if we build on the skills children are already learning. *Between the ages of two and five,* children are developing many capabilities that make the teaching of prevention skills possible. If your children are older than five, they already have these abilities; they just need to learn to recognize and respect them.

Children develop a sense of appropriate and inappropriate touching. Children gradually learn what kind of touch is common with different groups of people. It's expected that Mom and Dad will check their teeth after brushing, but it would be unusual to have a store clerk ask to check their teeth. Children readily accept hugs and kisses from family members. They respond differently to the same affection with someone they know less well. Children discriminate about touching early. They can learn to speak up when touching seems inappropriate.

Children have very clear ideas about what they like and don't like. Children know very early in life what they like and don't like, and they fully explore their ability to express these feelings during the "terrible twos." They discover that there is "yes" and there is "no." This is the time to begin teaching them that it is okay to speak up and how to do so.

Most children stop being so vocal by age four or five. Although they become more adapted and compliant, they should be encouraged to continue to express themselves. This doesn't mean they always get their way, but that they are heard.

Children can recognize and learn to respect their instinct. Children often "sense" that something is wrong before abuse actually occurs. When children learn to listen to their "inner voice" and to speak up, they are able to stop abuse before it even begins.

I remember the case of one young girl who had been molested by her uncle beginning when she was three. She told me about the day her uncle's "bouncing her on his lap" felt different from before. Although he was doing it with her parents in the room, and she kept looking at her mom and dad, they were not picking up on her unspoken plea for help.

Thinking no one cared, she didn't tell anyone about it and the abuse continued until she was twelve when she finally spoke up. But even at the age of three, she felt something was wrong and she knew she didn't like it. What she lacked was the ability and the skills to make it stop and to get help.

Unfortunately we don't always understand what children are trying to say. Your children may say to you, "Never, ever let that babysitter come back," but when you ask, "Why not?" they can't really explain or answer you. It makes sense to take time to draw them out, to get to the bottom of situations like that, because children sometimes intuitively sense that something is wrong but can't specifically describe what caused the feelings. You should pay heed to, and encourage your child to trust his or her natural alarm system. It deserves your respect. It is one of the most important tools for prevention of sexual abuse and abduction.

Such an approach to developing your child's innate protection skills is very different from trying to monitor touching for your children. For example, parents often express concern over children who are naturally affectionate, fearing that it makes them more vulnerable to abuse. We do not *want or need* to take away children's natural friendliness or affection. There is a great difference between affection and abuse; when touching crosses over from one to the other, children sense the difference. It's our responsibility to hear them when they tell us about it.

HOW TO USE THIS BOOK

This book has been written to help you teach your children to prevent sexual abuse and abduction. It will describe the problems and some solutions. A number of other books are listed in the bibliography that will help you follow-up with your children.

Use this book as a resource. Discuss and share it with the other adults in your children's lives such as teachers, grandparents, baby-sitters, neighbors, and friends. Prevention needs to be effective everywhere, and the more reinforcement your children get from other adults in their lives, the more successful they will be in keeping themselves safe.

Thinking about prevention begins when children are born, but actually teaching your children to take care of themselves really begins when they are between two and three years of age. The concepts of personal safety training in this book are applicable to children ages three through twelve. When the rules change or special problems arise for different ages, I will point it out to you.

Of the various techniques I suggest, the What If game is the most practical and instructive. Basically, it is a simple question-and-answer game that helps you and your children look at everyday situations in a new way. In fact, you probably already use it to some degree. For instance, what if the dog chews up this book before you

finish it? Although the What If questions are designed to teach your children about serious issues, they are presented in a light and non-threatening manner. Use it, enjoy it, adapt it to the places and situations in your own life.

The fundamentals of personal safety training should be taught carefully and thoughtfully, as you would teach swimming, crossing the street, or riding a bicycle. Once mastered, they are skills that can help to keep children safe. As children get older, the rules can change as their needs change. Consistent reinforcement and ongoing discussion about personal safety are the keys to long-term personal safety for your children.

Personal safety training, prevention of abuse, and prevention of abduction are delicate subjects to talk about, and you may feel that you've made mistakes in dealing with them. Don't be hard on yourself. Just let your children know that you have some new ideas and rules you'd like to discuss with them. Most children are astonishingly receptive to this simple approach.

Because most abuse and abduction of children occurs when you're not there to help, the most effective thing you can do is train your children to protect themselves. The prevention techniques I will describe have many practical applications. All in all, prevention is possible when you begin from what your children know, from what they've already experienced, from the natural abilities I have just described. From there, you build not only your children's sense of self-confidence in their ability to take care of themselves, but real skills that actually make them safer.

In addition, when you know—because you've played the games and talked about the rules—that your children can handle themselves in a wide variety of situations, you'll find it is easier to let go as they get older, and as it is appropriate. When you know your children have the ability to take care of themselves when they need to, it is possible for you to allow them the freedom of movement they need to be healthy, confident, and safe.

CHAPTER 2
The What If Game

What If is a teaching game that uses your children's spontaneous questions or your own What If questions as a springboard for discussion. By encouraging your children to talk about their thoughts, and by discussing your own reactions and ideas to a What If question, you and your children can agree on a possible resolution to that question. The game originates with any and all questions that begin with what if. It can be played any time, anyplace, and can cover any subject.

We all use the What If game to practice for the things we can anticipate in life, we just haven't given it a name. For example, we might ask ourselves: "What if my boss calls me on the carpet at the meeting tomorrow?" "What if we won the lottery?" "What if I'd hit that rabbit when the children were in the car?"

It is important that you understand the changes involved in adapting the game for children and how to play it with them so it works most effectively as a teaching tool. It will be used to establish your family rules and to teach all the personal safety skills discussed in this book. *The What If game helps children to anticipate and plan. It is this aspect of the game that makes it the single most valuable tool you have for teaching safety to your children.*

> **The purpose for any What If game is to:**
> ▶ **find out what your children think**
> ▶ **talk about possible solutions to a problem**
> ▶ **agree on one solution that seems the best and, from that, to establish working guidelines for what you or your children would do in such a situation**

A WINDOW INTO YOUR CHILDREN'S MINDS

Children ask What If questions that reflect their own fears, concerns, anxieties, and curiosities. Children are constantly exposed to reports of situations experienced by other people, which they then apply to themselves. For example, they see the story of a missing or kidnapped child on the news. They add to, subtract from, embellish, and endlessly modify the details of this story in an effort to understand, rationalize, and experience some sense of control should such a thing ever happen to them. The game is an opportunity for them to explore ideas as they think and talk about all the ways they might handle the situation.

Children often translate these thoughts into What If questions and reactions. They might say ''What if I had been playing in my yard when that kidnapper came around? I'd have run away. No, I'd have popped him in the mouth.''

If you can resist the urge to answer and instead let your children answer the What If questions first, you will discover how they think, what their concerns are, how they solve problems, how they think the world works, and what they know and don't

know about keeping themselves safe. Adults answer children's questions, assuming that obtaining information is why they asked. But that isn't always the case. When you give children all the answers, you deny them the opportunity to confront and resolve their own questions.

By listening instead, you get accurate information about your children's concerns. They can ask difficult or "silly" questions in the What If game without feeling embarrassed or foolish, and they can talk about their feelings and experiences without increasing their own anxiety. Most important of all, your children can use the What If game to report an incident they might otherwise keep secret.

Children often don't tell about something that has happened to them because they don't want to upset anyone. In the game, children can pretend it didn't happen, even though it did. Because it's only a "what if," it's a bit like make-believe, and some of the emotional sting is reduced. There is no basis for you to get upset by such a question, and your child can find out what you will do, how you will react, and then decide whether or not he or she wants to admit what happened.

Getting Started

Children can initiate the What If game by simply asking a question that begins with what if. In my experience I have found that most children do this. I remember a father whose son kept asking "What if there's no food in the house?" The father replied they'd go to the store. His son then asked, "Well, what if there's no food at the store?" The father's answer generated another question, and on and on.

The next time they played the game, things went very differently. When his son asked "What if there's no food in the house?" the father responded with "That's a good question, what do you think?" With that opening the child was able to talk about his real concern, which was that his father was unemployed and he wanted to know what they'd do when they ran out of food and money.

If your children don't ask What If questions, you can introduce the What If game by saying, "What If the dog ran away?" or "What If mommy was in the shower and the telephone rang?"

Once the What If game is started, rather than answer the questions yourself, let your children find the answers independently. For example, in response to a younger child's question you could say something like:

> *"That's a really good question, what do you think?" or "Gee, I haven't thought about that, what do you think?" or "I have some ideas about that, but I'd really like to know what you think first."*

For older children, you might respond with:

> *"I'd like to hear what you think about that" or "I don't really know exactly what I'd do, what do you think?"*

Some children will balk at going first and put the burden on you. If your child really wants you to go first, do so. After a few What If games, you can begin to take turns by reminding your child "I went first last time."

Remember, it *is* a game. Avoid making an issue over any part of it or the value will be lost. The What If game is not a confrontation. It is an opportunity to share ideas and initiate discussion.

THE WHAT IF GAME SHOULD NEVER FRIGHTEN

Since the idea of the What If game is to teach skills without *adding* to the fears and anxieties your children may already have, parents should ask questions that create no *new* fears or anxieties for children. Start with a What If example your children have already expressed. For instance, most children are afraid they might get lost in a shopping center, at a stadium, or in some other crowded place. The illustrated example is an ideal way to get started.

The most enjoyable way to illustrate a What If game such as this one is to role-play, or act out, the actual situation. You can portray a variety of characters: a cashier, a well-meaning friend or customer, and a "grumpy" store manager. It is important that your children realize that *these are not bad people, especially the "grumpy" store manager.* Your children can play themselves and learn through the

What if we were at the new shopping center together and you looked around and couldn't find me? What do you think you'd do?

I'd look for you and if I couldn't find you, I'd find a police officer and go to the police station.

Could you go to the person at the first cash register you, see and tell her you're lost?

I could go and say that my mom and dad are lost.

Okay. So you'd go to the cash register and say you're lost. Could you do something else for me? Could you stay right in that spot and not move until I come to get you?

I'd stay right there.

What if someone bothered you or tried to make you go with him?

I could hit and kick him.

role-plays to say no and to stick to it, even in the face of an adult who seems threatening or physically tries to take them somewhere.

In real life, this process will not go quite so quickly or smoothly. Play with your children's ideas. Recognize that children have a great resistance to saying they'd scream—probably because they're taught not to scream in a store. The object is to establish what they should do and to practice it.

Even when you are role-playing and pretending to take them away, I cannot emphasize strongly enough that your children should never feel frightened or insecure. The game should not be alarming. Play gently; be silly and reassuring.

The What If game I have just described sounds like it is about children getting lost and what they should do. In fact, in playing this game, you are teaching abduction prevention. At the same time you're talking about being lost you're teaching your children what to do and what to say should they be asked or forced to go with someone. What's important to note is that you can teach abduction prevention without ever mentioning abduction and without frightening your children.

Through the game, your children experience that by being assertive, they can handle a difficult situation successfully and that you will support and praise them for sticking to their guns.

SPECIAL ISSUES FOR CHILDREN OF DIFFERENT AGES

Three- to Six-year-olds

Preschoolers and kindergartners play the What If game with enthusiasm. I am always astonished at the range and diversity of their concerns. They are not the carefree spirits we sometimes imagine they are, but rather are complex individuals with their own private fears and worries.

Recognizing that your young children have concerns about their own safety is actually an *opportunity* for you. Because of their receptivity to new ideas, this is the ideal time for your children to learn that they can take care of themselves and that you sometimes want them to do so.

The sort of questions even preschoolers might ask include: "What if you didn't come to pick me up and everyone went home?" or "What if my teacher said I could go home with her?" or "What if you fell down and hurt your head and someone came to the door?"

Seven- to Nine-year-olds

Seven- to nine-year-olds are the most vulnerable group for abuse. They have more freedom to come and go—walking to school, running errands, shopping alone, and so on. At the same time, they often feel insecure about what to do in new situations. At this age they are also beginning to feel their parents are not listening, are not interested, or might not believe them if they come to them with a problem. Specific preparation through the What If game is needed to reduce the risk that goes along with the increased freedom of children in this age group.

These children also have the most distorted perceptions about what they can do to solve problems. They sometimes have what I call a karate mentality. They believe they will "karate chop" their way to safety. While these fantasies are natural and healthy, they should be tempered with a clear distinction between reality and make-believe. This is most easily accomplished by demonstration.

Adults are bigger and stronger. If your children believe they can keep themselves safe by physical power, simply demonstrate that in real life, it's not so. Safety comes from a real understanding of what works and what doesn't work. This is one of the most important distinctions children can learn at this age.

Ten- to Twelve-year-olds

Children ten and up are more easily embarrassed, and they increasingly assume that their parents do not believe them or take them seriously. The What If game is particularly important for this group. For example, to check your reactions, your child might ask, "What if I heard that my friend John was invited to join a shoplifting club?" or "What if the other kids got caught smoking in the bathroom and I was there?"

Embarrassment, peer pressure, and a developing sense of independence are the primary factors that keep children ages ten to twelve from communicating with their parents. These personal pressures can literally prevent your children from being able to get out of a dangerous situation. The What If game may seem immature and silly to preteens, but it can be revised to make it more effective.

Let them take the lead, listen more than you talk, and pay attention to any underlying theme in what they're saying. This is particularly true if the scenario is one step removed by suggesting that it is really their friend who wants to know what to do. For example, when your daughter says, "Molly was wondering what she should do if a boy tries to kiss her, but she doesn't want to ask her mom," she is probably asking about herself.

This technique of asking a question for a friend often leads to the discovery of sexual abuse cases. For example, after one of my classes, two girls came up with a number of theoretical questions about adults who were threatening friends of theirs. On the basis of my answers, which were honest and nonjudgmental, one of them decided to tell me about her own abuse and asked my help in reporting. Her decision to tell was based on my answers to their What If questions.

Preteens don't want to expose their vulnerability, their insecurities, and their attempts to be more grown up. They try to solve situations themselves rather than asking for help. It is essential that your family develop a way of handling the conflict between a preteen's desire for privacy and independence and his or her need to acquire problem-solving skills.

WHAT IFS—HOW PARENTS INITIATE AND PLAY

While the What If game should be played mostly in response to your children's questions, there are also questions you will want to initiate. When you want to ask a question, try to present examples that teach your children what to do without producing fear or anxiety. Serious concerns can be dealt with by a "silly" or "fun" question.

For example, your children can learn that it's all right for them to say no to requests from adults without your making generalities that can lead them to conclude that all adults are bad. The concept is learned by "silly" questions, but the examples are real enough that your children learn they can say no. To teach this you might say:

"What if your teacher said, 'Today we're all going to take our shoes and socks off and go out and play in the snow'?" Children will laugh and say, "Of course I wouldn't go, I'd catch a cold."

When you're thinking of a question you want to ask your children, ask it to yourself first. If you think the question will create any fear or anxiety for your children, ask it some other way. An *inappropriate* question might sound like this: "What if someone came and snatched your baby sister out of the front yard when you were taking care of her? What would you do?" This type of question creates a new fear rather than teaching prevention. It would be better to ask "What if you were in the yard with your baby sister and someone you didn't know came into the yard? What would you do?"

We don't have the right to project our own fears onto our children. It is always possible to ask your question in a way that is fun and instructive. If you know the skill you want to teach, as in the example just given, ask a general question, that is, one with no specific details or descriptions. This will allow you to determine whether or not your children can handle the specific situation about which you are concerned. It is also instructive because children can and will generalize from it.

Asking What If questions that are *too* specific can be equally misleading. Overly specific questions don't allow children to extend the example to other occurrences. They teach children to watch out only for that particular situation. Using appropriately general examples allows for expansion to include any specific situation and creates no new fear.

DON'T ASK:	DO ASK:
What if you were walking home from school and a big white van pulled up and a man wearing a cowboy hat tried to make you get into his car?	What if you were walking home from school and you saw a car or person who seemed suspicious or that you felt funny about?
This is teaching children to watch out for white cars and cowboy hats.	*This is not frightening or so detailed that children can visualize a specific danger. It teaches an overall skill that can be applied in any particular situation.*

DON'T ASK:

What if your baby-sitter asked you to take down your pants and let him touch your penis?

This introduces an image your children may never specifically have thought of and the new anxiety that goes along with it.

DO ASK:

What if your baby-sitter touched you in a way you didn't like?

This generic question allows you to talk about the concept without giving your children more information than they need.

DON'T ASK:

What if someone broke a window and came into your bedroom with a gun when you were home alone?

This is unnecessarily frightening.

DO ASK:

What if you were home by yourself and you thought you heard someone in the house?

This is something children think about. The tone of your questions should be matter-of-fact.

When the What If game becomes a regular part of your family's discussions, your children can talk about fears and anxieties as they come up, rather than privately worrying about them. For example, a six-year-old girl was abducted from a playground outside Denver. Her death and the ensuing media coverage created enormous anxiety for all the schoolchildren in the area. In spite of the tragic circumstances, the situation provided an opportunity for parents to discuss in a positive way what their children could do if someone approached them. The object of the What If game is to help children feel more secure and confident when they are worried.

Never respond to a What If question by saying "Oh, that'll never happen to you." When you say this, your children really hear "Mom and Dad don't want to talk about it," which only increases their concern. Instead of dismissing the question, recognize it as an opportunity to turn that fear into something your children can be comfortable discussing.

ONE ESSENTIAL WHAT IF QUESTION

What if something bad happens while children are doing something you've expressly forbidden? What do they do? They frequently don't tell anyone which is why we've created a special What If for this complicated situation. For example, if they go to someone's house without permission and are sexually abused, they may not tell because they'd first have to confess their own wrong doing and admit that they broke the rules. It is imperative that your children have a way to talk to you if something should happen under such circumstances—even when they feel guilty.

Children tend to feel at fault when anything bad happens. Even if they weren't doing anything wrong, they think they were. So if they were misbehaving, they especially believe they have caused the bad thing to happen to them.

In trying to protect children we can sometimes create the impression that getting hurt is a consequence of their own mistakes. For instance when we say "Well, if you hadn't been riding your bike so fast, you wouldn't have fallen off and cut your leg." This belief may unfortunately prevent a child from telling us they have been abused or hurt because they will be certain they did something to cause and/or deserve it.

It is possible to circumvent this problem in part by teaching children as young as preschoolers that *sometimes* bad things do just happen and they are not in any way to blame. One easy way to do this is to ask "Did you feel it was your fault?" when they get hurt. Cut knees and broken toys are opportunities to talk about your child's sense of guilt or blame in what happened.

In order for your children to tell you what has happened to them in spite of breaking the rules, they must know what they can expect from you. The following What If question should help:

> *"What if you go somewhere we've told you never to go and something bad happens? How will you tell me?"* or *"What if you go with someone we've told you never to go with and you get into trouble with them? Would you tell me?"*

Whatever their response is, follow with "If something like that happened, we'd want to know because we love you and want you to be safe." Suggest that: "We'd take care of the bad thing that happened and you could decide what should happen because you broke the rules." In a real situation, they'll be a lot tougher on themselves than you'll ever be because you're just glad they're home and safe.

It is important that consequences be established for children's misbehavior under these circumstances. Otherwise they make the mistake of thinking that the bad thing that happened to them was their punishment. The consequences for their misbehavior should be natural or logical—that is, they should have something to do with the misbehavior. They should be set without moral judgment or anger, and your child should feel that he or she has learned something from what happened.

WHEN CHILDREN ASK QUESTIONS REPEATEDLY

Occasionally children get stuck and repeatedly ask the same question. Usually the problem is simply that the real question, the source of the child's concern, is not being addressed. When this happens, the question should be broken down into smaller, more workable, pieces until you discover the real issue.

The most telling illustration I've had of this problem involved a five-year-old who, after the fire department visited her school, kept asking "What if there was a fire in the house?" Her mother carefully discussed the safety procedures and drew fire escape routes, which were then tacked on the walls. All to no avail. The child continued to repeat her question.

When her mother called me, I suggested she turn the question back and ask "What if there was a fire in the house, what do you think would be the biggest problems?" or "What would be the hardest part?"

A week later the mother called to say that her turning the question around had released a flood of specific queries about what would happen to toys, blankets, school books, and other treasures in a fire. Each of these concerns was listened to, addressed, and after a few days her daughter relaxed and the questions stopped. The initial question "What if there is a fire in the house?" had not been the real one. Only by getting to the real question was the child reassured.

Older children, around nine or ten, tend to stop asking questions if you don't pick up on their underlying concerns. That's why the What If game format in which they talk first really serves the purpose of ensuring that you know your child's concern *before* you make your suggestions.

WHAT IF CHECKLIST

▶ Your children should ask most of the What If questions.

▶ Do not ask questions that alarm or frighten your children.

▶ Use role-playing or acting out as a way to make the game more fun and to firmly establish the expected behavior.

▶ Never respond to your children's What If question by saying "Oh, don't worry about that. That'll never happen to you."

▶ Be aware of age differences when playing the What If game so older children aren't insulted or turned off.

▶ If your children keep asking the same thing over and over, recognize that that isn't the question they really want answered.

▶ Make sure your children know in advance what the consequences will be of telling you something that happened during some kind of misbehavior.

CHAPTER 3
Understanding Sexual Abuse

As much as we try to protect and care for our children, we simply are not present to prevent sexual abuse ourselves. Therefore, prevention means preparing your children to recognize potential abuse, and to stop an assault at its inception. Training gives your children the ability to do that, even with someone who is older, more knowledgeable, more powerful, or much loved by them. Prevention training tells them what they need to know and assures them that you are there to believe and help them if something happens.

Prevention of sexual abuse can be taught without talking about sexual abuse. Children don't need to be told what sexual abuse is, who perpetrators are, how they operate, what they do or why. Children don't need a list of ways in which they might be abused. Instead, children must acquire the ability to make decisions for themselves based on what they feel to be true at that moment. They must have permission to speak up. They need specific techniques to stop what's being done to them. And they must know they will be believed and supported by the adults in their lives.

Parents, on the other hand, do need to understand the nature of sexual abuse. The prevention techniques I will present are based on the patterns and techniques of abusers. The more you know about what sexual abuse is, who abuses children, how they operate, and why children become involved, the more effectively you can teach prevention to your children.

WHAT IS SEXUAL ABUSE?

Sexual abuse is legally defined as any sexual contact with a child or the use of a child for the sexual gratification of someone else. It includes exhibitionism, child pornography, fondling of the genitals or asking the child to do so, oral sex, and attempts to penetrate the vagina or anus. Of all of these, fondling is the most common form of sexual abuse.

Parents often ask whether exhibitionism is really harmful. For some children it is, for others it is not. The answer lies in the child's perception. If a child feels frightened, out of control, and violated, the exhibitionism should be considered abusive. If the child is matter-of-fact about it, it may not have been damaging for him or her. This does not mean it's not a crime. It just means it wasn't upsetting to the child.

The insidious, complex, and sordid nature of the child sexual abuse cases now being revealed is astonishing, even for those of us who see it daily. *While we read about the spectacular cases, the greater majority of sexual abuse incidents quietly occur between the child and someone he or she trusts with no physical injury or life-threatening acts.* It is this "quiet" nature of sexual abuse that makes it so hard to recognize, so hard to believe, and so hard to accept.

WHY SEXUAL ABUSE IS SO DESTRUCTIVE

The physical things that happen to children who are sexually abused are often damaging, but the greatest long-term injury to children comes from their sense of betrayal by the person who abused them. The more important the relationship, the bigger the betrayal and loss, especially when the abuse occurs with a parent or grandparent. This betrayal is compounded if the child tells and is not believed or the abuse is not stopped.

Sexually abused children feel a loss of control; they feel victimized and uncertain about whom to trust. This emotional damage is far more long-lasting than the physical effects and requires careful, nurturing support and counseling to repair.

WHO ARE THE PERPETRATORS?

We don't know nearly enough about who commits child sexual abuse or why they do what they do. But what we do know is shocking.

Sexual abusers of children, first and foremost, are almost always individuals who were sexually abused as children, although many do not remember the experience until they are in treatment. They are people who were victimized, who did not receive sufficient help in recovering from their own abuse, and who deal with what happened to them, in part, by abusing children.

Some basic facts:

▶ Pedophilia is the term for sexual preference for children.

▶ It has nothing to do with homosexuality.

► Some pedophiles prefer girls, some prefer boys, and some have no preference.

► Eighty-five to 90% of all sexual abuse takes place with someone the child knows and trusts.

► In 1979 David Finkelhor reported that 26% of sexual abuse takes place with a family member, including parents, grandparents, siblings, aunts, uncles, and stepparents.

► While most pedophiles are men, Finkelhor's research indicates that at least 10 percent of all perpetrators are female.

► Gene Abel and Judith Becker reported that the average molestor of girl children will molest 62 victims and the average molestor of boy children will molest 30 victims. It is for this reason that we often find them in positions of trust where they have access to children.

Sexual abuse of children is a way of life for many of these individuals. Their abuse of children may begin immediately after their own experience. Other times it lies dormant until midlife, when they become sexually involved with children. Whenever it begins, their abuse of children comes from the damage inflicted upon them as children. It is a continuation of the cycle where those who are abused go on to abuse others. This is not to say that all victims become pedophiles. They don't. But all victims are potential abusers until they can get adequate care and treatment.

The motivations of these individuals are many but basically, the 85–90% who abuse children they know are seeking an intimate, nonjudgmental, affectionate relationship with a child. *They need to exercise power and control over children and to believe that children "willingly" enter, if not initiate and encourage, the sexual relationships.* These perpetrators are often, without knowing it, seeking to resolve their own childhood abuse experience. Because they are "victims" themselves, they rarely believe or understand that what they are doing "hurts" children.

There is no profile available that can help you identify potential abusers. They tend to be people we like and trust, and their obvious and genuine care for children earns them our admiration. This, in part, explains why it is so very difficult for us to accept how badly we misjudged someone when he or she is discovered and how difficult it is for our children to tell us what happened.

INCEST

Incest is unquestionably the most difficult kind of sexual abuse for parents to think about. Unless you have experienced it, it is *unthinkable* that someone who is a part of your family would violate your child's trust and love in this way. Nevertheless, in one of the most comprehensive studies to date, Diana Russell found that 16 percent of the women participating in her study had experienced sexual abuse with a family member at least five years older. Father/daughter incest was reported by 4.5 percent of the women.

While the nature of the problem seems vastly different, the prevention techniques described in this book are designed to prevent incest as well as abuse by other people known to the child. It is not appropriate to suggest to children that members of their family would sexually abuse them. As a parent, however, you should know that you will be teaching techniques to help prevent incest.

STEPPARENTS AS ABUSERS

In her 1981 report Diana Russell also confirms that stepfathers are much more likely than biological fathers to sexually abuse their stepdaughters. Knowing this, women who have boyfriends and/or subsequently new husbands should prepare their children differently for prevention of sexual abuse.

This is a very difficult problem. Boyfriends and stepfathers hold an influential position with children. They know that children want their mothers to be happy and, if they are abusers, they often tell the child that they will abandon the mother if the child doesn't cooperate. Children go along rather than create upheaval. They don't want to be responsible for their mothers' relationship breaking up.

Preparing children means talking to them about what they should do if your boyfriend or their stepfather asks them to do something they know they shouldn't do. Talk about the difference between respect and blind obedience. Let your children know that you will never stop loving them and they they can always come to you if they are uncomfortable with something being said or done to them by someone else. In teaching the prevention techniques described in this book, be sure your children know they apply to *everyone*.

DO CHILDREN ABUSE ONE ANOTHER?

I get a lot of calls from parents who wonder if their children have been sexually abused by a playmate. *When children are abused, they sometimes reenact what happened to them with one of their peers.* If this pattern is repeated by subsequent children, it can create a situation in which a number of them repeat sexual play that is both inappropriate and confusing. This is not so much a case of rampant sexual abuse as a situation requiring reeducation of the children so they can find more appropriate ways to play with one another. In all cases, every effort should be made to discover the perpetrator who sexually abused the first child.

PLAYING DOCTOR

Observing sexual play is one of the common ways we discover sexual abuse in young children. Normally, playing doctor is mutual and healthy exploration and play. It never includes one child victimizing another, nor does it include oral-genital contact or attempts to penetrate the vagina or anus. If you come across suspicious play, simply ask, "What game are you playing?" "Who else plays this game with you?" "How do you play this game?" Children will often tell you

exactly where they learned this "game," and you can immediately find out whether or not there is a problem.

In all events, it is essential that you not "overreact" in such a situation. All children play doctor. If that's the situation you've come upon, use it as an opportunity to initiate discussion and give guidelines. Children want to know about themselves and others. During the preschool years especially, when children are open, if not matter-of-fact, about their bodies, answer their questions. At the same time, you can establish that you know it feels good to touch themselves and that it's all right to do so in private. It is not okay to touch others or ask them to touch you.

THE TOOLS OF THE CHILD ABUSER

Friendship, trust, and bribery are the most common and effective tools of the abuser. Abusers take time to get to know children and to develop relationships with them. At some point they initiate the sexual abuse act or, quite commonly, they "test" to see if this is a child who will participate. For example, they might stick their hand up the child's shirt while tickling or wrestling. Or they might ask the child to sit close to them while riding in the car and rest their hand on the child's inner thigh. *These are not inherently abusive activities, but they do test a child's ability to be assertive in a situation that is uncomfortable.*

When a child resists, perpetrators often respond with "Don't you like me?" "Don't you love me?" "Don't you want to be my friend?"

In effect, they are using their relationship with the child to obtain his or her compliance. This, combined with the abuser's greater power, knowledge, and experience, tips the balance against the child, and most give in. If, on the other hand, a child has learned prevention skills and is firm about stopping the behavior, the perpetrator will generally move on to another, less resistant child.

WHY CHILDREN LET IT CONTINUE

Being smaller and more trusting, children often buy the assurances of their "friend" and allow the uncomfortable activity to continue. This encourages the perpetrator, and the abuse quickly escalates. Once this happens, it is very difficult for children to extricate themselves. In my experience, the four primary concerns that keep children from telling are guilt, close relationship, fear they won't be believed or that telling will cause too much disruption.

Guilt always accompanies sexual abuse. Children say to themselves, "If something bad happened to my body and I didn't stop it, then I must be bad or it must be my fault. And it happened with someone I liked a lot."

Children, in spite of their abuse, continue to value the relationship they have with the abuser and recognize that it would be lost if they reveal the truth. This is a powerful factor and should not be forgotten after the abuse is discovered. Many children, and even parents, will continue to feel protective toward the abuser after the abuse has been revealed, especially if the perpetrator is a family member.

Children fear that they won't be believed if they do tell someone. This is very real, particularly when the abuser is someone loved and trusted by the family or the community. They may also fear that someone will be hurt if they tell. Finally, they may feel that they are protecting other children from becoming victims by allowing the abuse to continue.

Children very perceptively recognize or are convinced by the abuser that telling could create family disruption, possible divorce, court appearances, jail, and so on. In letting the abuse continue, children often feel they are protecting the ones they love.

DO CHILDREN LIE ABOUT SEXUAL ABUSE?

Almost without exception, children do not lie about sexual abuse, except to deny that it happened. If a child can describe what happened, you must believe that it did indeed occur. This does not mean that children may not misinterpret or misreport an event. But because children don't normally have access to descriptions of sexual activities, it's not really possible for them to "make up" or "fantasize" sexual abuse. Children who can talk about their abuse in detail have experienced it.

As children learn more about sexual abuse—particularly from the media—parents and professionals are concerned that false reports will increase, particularly with preadolescents and adolescents. While this is definitely a possibility, the child who is fabricating reports of sexual abuse can be quickly unmasked by an experienced interviewer. Sexual abuse of children has been underreported for so long that the possibility of false reports is small compared to the enormity of the actual problem.

Children, in fact, more often than not tell us without meaning to. For example, if you see your children "playing sex" (not playing doctor), if you get a "French kiss" good night, if you suddenly hear new names for body parts or see sexually provocative behavior, no matter how alarmed or upset you feel, you should calmly ask "Who taught you that?" "Who else plays that game with you?" *Any time a child can answer these questions and talk about a sexual abuse experience, you must believe it happened, even if he or she gets scared and tells you a few hours later that the story was made up.*

SEX ABUSE AND SEX EDUCATION

Training in the prevention of sexual abuse is not the same as sex education. I do believe, however, that understanding his or her body is important to a child's positive self-image and that it can help reduce the child's vulnerability to exploitation and abuse.

It is important to use accurate names for body parts as a way of teaching healthy respect for our bodies. It is customary in our society to use pet names or nicknames for the genitalia. This may be Victorian, or it may be an attempt by parents to "protect" their children's innocence, or it may be a simple continuation of how our parents taught us. Whatever the reason, we don't nickname our eyes or ears or toes, and we should not do it with other body parts either.

The fact is that children who think there is something "secret" or "different" about their genital area are more vulnerable to suggestions that they are "bad" for very normal kinds of play, such as masturbation. This suggestion of "badness" can be a powerful weapon in the hands of a perpetrator. Being comfortable and at ease with their body is a simple and natural beginning for abuse-prevention training for children.

CHAPTER 4
Preventing Sexual Abuse

Prevention of sexual abuse training begins with your children's natural abilities, what they already know, and the experiences they've already had. It is built on conveying the following ideas effectively to your children early on:

▶ **Your body belongs to you**

▶ **You have a right to say who touches you and how**

▶ **If someone touches you in a way you don't like, in a way that makes you feel funny or uncomfortable inside, or in a way that you think is wrong, it's okay to say no**

▶ **If the person doesn't stop, you say, "I'm going to tell" and then you tell, no matter what**

▶ **If you're asked to keep a secret, you say, "No, I'm going to tell."**

▶ **If you have a problem, keep talking about it until someone helps you**

YOUR BODY BELONGS TO YOU

Children learn they have control over what happens to their body when we teach them, and when we show them by our own behavior, that their body does indeed belong to them. This is a new idea to preschoolers who may think their bodies are our property because we're always taking care of them.

Many children tell me that their body belongs to God. I suggest to them that they are partners with God. Children help God to take care of them by taking care of their body, brushing their hair, dressing themselves, and keeping themselves safe.

Simply, as the first step in prevention, you can say to your children:

"Your body belongs to you. You have a right to say who touches you and how. If someone touches you in a way you don't like, in a way that makes you feel funny or uncomfortable or in a way you think is wrong, it's okay to say 'No, stop it' and that person should stop."

Illustrate this by recalling times when your children have been touched in ways they didn't like or felt uncomfortable about: when Aunt Sally pinches their cheek, when next-door neighbor Fred throws them over his head, when big sister tickles and won't stop, or when a friend of Dad's hugs too hard. What's new is that it's okay to say no.

Obviously, none of these examples constitute sexual abuse. However, when children learn to say no to someone who pinches their cheek, or picks them up, they learn to say no to more intrusive, harmful touching.

How to Say No

Your children already know what touching they like and what touching they don't like. Touching they don't like makes them feel uneasy and seems wrong to them. You are simply giving them permission to be assertive and teaching them how to speak up, in a way that is acceptable. It's important to help your children find the words and to practice so they can say them, without hesitation, in a clear, audible voice. Give them lots of ways to say no. Here are some examples:

> *"Please stop, I don't like that."*
> or *"That's not fun anymore, and I don't want you to do it."*
> or *"Leave me alone."*
> or *"You shouldn't be asking me to do that, leave me alone."*
> or *"I'm not allowed to do things like that, please take me home now."* or simply *"Stop."*

Verbal messages alone are not enough. Your children must also show with their body what they want to say. I frequently have children in my classes who are saying "Don't hug me so hard" as they are climbing up on my lap. Children should learn to say no with their body by moving away at the same time they are saying no with their words.

Examples for Three- to Six-year-olds

Young children tell me that some of the ways they don't like to be touched are: kisses on the mouth, getting their shirts tucked in by grown-ups, being picked up, having their hair stroked, having to kiss Grandma and Grandpa or Mom and Dad's friends. All of these are contacts or touch that adults take for granted. For children, they are sometimes okay; other times they can be unwanted touch, just as sexual abuse is unwanted touch. Whether we agree or not, it is important to respect children's preferences. By learning to say no to one type of touching children learn to say no to the other.

One class of preschoolers demonstrated this brilliantly. I had just completed an exercise with a little girl who said she didn't like to be kissed on the lips. As the girl sat down a little boy stood up, looked for his mother in the back of the room, and said, "Mom, I really love you, but I don't want to be kissed on the lips anymore, I want to be kissed on the cheek." He already knew he didn't like to be kissed on the lips; what I had given him was permission to speak his mind and the words to do so. He wasn't passing up the opportunity.

One of the things you can add, after your children begin to get the idea, is "If someone tries to touch your body, or asks you to touch theirs, or to do things that you don't do with anyone else, don't let them, especially if they want you to keep it secret. Come and tell me."

PRIVATE PARTS

Too much emphasis can be placed on private parts. Most abusers don't begin their abuse with the private parts, so prevention is a little late by the time they do. *It is appropriate, however, to discuss the private parts of the body as a part of the prevention training.*

Private parts include the genital area, the buttocks, and the breasts. It's sometimes easier for parents to say something like "The parts of your body that your bathing suit and underwear cover up are special parts of your body. You can touch yourself there, but other people shouldn't, except if you're sick or at the doctor. Those same parts of the body are special for other people and it's not okay for someone older than you to touch you or to ask you to touch their private parts, especially if they ask you to keep it a secret."

EXAMPLES FOR SEVEN- TO TWELVE-YEAR-OLDS

As children get older, examples of intrusive touch are harder to discuss because of the increasingly complex emotions that affect their relationships. Peer pressure, the need for approval and acceptance, and embarrassment all become more important as children get older. Offenders know this, and skillfully manipulate and exploit these emotions.

The following examples can help you teach your school-age children to confront and deal with emotionally complex situations rather than avoid them or tolerate them with increasing discomfort.

▶ *What if your teacher always puts her arm around you when you come up to the front of the room and you like it? But today is different because you missed almost all of the words on your spelling test and you're upset. So, when she puts her arm around you, you pull away. She pulls you closer. You pull away again and say, "Leave me alone." She doesn't understand and says, "What's bugging you?" loud enough for the other kids to hear. What do you do?*

How about saying softly, "I missed almost all the words on my spelling test, I'm crabby and don't want you to put your arm around me?" She can respect your wishes if she understands.

▶ *What if your dad's still giving you big bear hugs, but your breasts are developing and his bear hugs are embarrassing and it hurts? How do you tell him?*

I could probably talk to Dad for you to help you let him know you still love him, but bear hugs are out for a while.

▶ *What if your soccer coach hits you on the arm every time he gets near you on the field? The other guys don't seem to mind, but you hate it and ask him to stop. The next day he does it again. You turn to him and tell him to keep his hands to himself. His response is "You don't like it, get off the team." What do you do?*

(The vast majority of children will solve this problem by quitting the team, which is too bad because the problem is with the coach, not with the child.)

Let's say you decide to tell your dad. When you do, your dad asks what you did that caused the coach to hit you. When you say "Nothing," your dad says the coach wouldn't hit you for nothing. So you show your dad how he hits you. Then your dad responds with "Oh, that's part of being on the team and it means the coach likes you." Did Dad understand your problem? Now what do you do? How about telling your uncle? Maybe he can help talk to your dad. Just because "everyone does it," you don't have to go along.

While these situations are not sexual abuse, the examples help children learn how to deal effectively with problems that are emotionally complex. These stories are similar to the dilemmas children face in actual sexual abuse situations. One of the things we're teaching children is to *keep talking*, keep telling until someone hears, understands their problem, and helps. Encourage your children to use the What If game to reinforce and practice telling when it seems no one is listening.

DOUBLE MESSAGES

These are basic concepts, familiar to many parents, and they seem pretty simple and straightforward. I'd like to illustrate, however, how difficult it can be to change the way we behave toward children with the following situations:

▶ You're in the grocery store with your preschooler and a friend approaches. Your child immediately hides behind your legs. You urge him to come out and talk to your friend.

▶ Gram and Gramp come over for dinner. When they're leaving they want a kiss. Your child says no. You suggest that Gram and Gramp drove a long way, or Gram and Gramp love her very much, or they might not come next week if they don't get a kiss.

▶ You want a good-night kiss. Your child says no. You ask, "Don't you love me?" or "Are you mad at me?"

▶ A friend of the family has hugs and kisses for everyone after a long vacation. Your child resists and your response is "You know we haven't seen her for a long time, you don't want to hurt her feelings."

In all of these situations, what we're saying to children is that adults' feelings are more important than their own, that they should suppress their own feelings to please adults. If they don't, they're not being "good" children. Even if the message is unintended, it is what children hear.

This distinction is important because this kind of hidden message is very similar to what perpetrators say when children resist sexual abuse. "Don't you like me?", "Don't you love me?", "Don't you want to be my friend?" are all examples of coercive questions. Because of the way children interpret our words and actions, they don't know that it is absolutely all right to say no and to stick to it no matter what emotional ploys are used to change their minds.

How Should Adults Respond?

When children express uneasiness about any kind of touching, you can reassure them by saying "Thank you for telling me you don't like that. I'll try to remember," or "You know, grown-ups can't read your mind. I'm glad you told me to stop," or "It's okay to say no, even if I'm a grown-up."

Note that we aren't labeling any behavior or touching as "good" touching or "bad" touching. We don't want to create any controversy about touching or to confuse children by categorizing touch. We are simply leaving decisions about touching up to them.

With all this discussion about touching, it is important to remind children of all the touches they enjoy, saying something such as "If you like it, it's probably okay." One of the myths about child sexual abuse is that children enjoy it or that it feels good. This is not true. On the few occasions when it does feel good, the abuse is accompanied by many uncomfortable and uneasy feelings. In the beginning stages of sexual abuse, children are not fooled about what is happening because it feels good.

Letting Children Decide

More and more, I'm hearing fathers express uncertainty about how they should play with their children, how they should express affection. All the publicity about child abuse has made them almost fearful about touching their own children. The answer is: *Just as you always have*, adding only an awareness of the need to be responsive and to reinforce your child's expression of his or her likes and dislikes.

One father described the day he was playing at the pool with his three-year-old daughter. Her shrieks of delight were misinterpreted by several people who thought she was protesting. He stopped playing the game with her, but he was also angry that his relationship with her was being changed by the opinions of others.

Prevention of abuse does not include changing your behaviors. Children need all the love, affection, and nurturing you can give them. **One of the worst possible consequences of abuse-prevention training would be the withdrawal of normal adult affection and play with children.** Prevention is based on allowing children to decide about touching for themselves and giving them permission and support to speak up for themselves.

I'M GOING TO TELL

Once you recognize that the vast majority of abusers are known to the child and that seeming compliance on the child's part is necessary to the successful completion of the offense, you can see that simple resistance is a powerful prevention tool. "I'm going to tell" is the second step for children to extricate themselves from a difficult situation or to avoid a sexual assault.

Your children need to be taught to say "I don't like that" or "stop it" or "leave me alone" or some variation of no any time they're being touched in a way that's not okay with them. They then need to learn to say, "I'm going to tell if you don't leave me alone" immediately if their first request is ignored. Rather than risk being found out, perpetrators who are known to the child usually back off when their efforts to persuade the child prove futile.

Parents often ask me: "If my child says no, will he [or she] get hurt?" Most will not. Remember that abusers are looking for a warm, nonjudgmental, affectionate relationship. They don't want or need rejection. In addition, it's easier for them to find another child than to risk discovery by hurting one who refuses to go along with them. In all cases, children must know that it's okay to tell what happened to them, even if they promised the abuser they wouldn't.

Children also need to be taught to tell their parents or someone they trust *anytime* they have to say "I'm going to tell" in order to get someone to stop touching them. And they most know that they will be believed and supported.

TATTLING

Children often confuse "I'm going to tell" with tattling. **Explain that tattling is telling on someone the same age as you, or a brother or sister, so you can get them in trouble.** When they smile at this definition, you know they know exactly what you mean.

Telling because they need help with a problem or because a friend needs help or because someone older is bugging them is *never* tattling. This is an easy and clear distinction for children to make when you give them a few examples.

▶ *What if Bobby's big brother was beating up on him all the time; would it be tattling for you to tell me about it?* No, because Bobby needs help.

▶ *What if someone at your school was stealing your lunch money; would it be tattling to tell your teacher about it?* No, because that's a problem you need help to solve.

▶ *What if the baby-sitter's boyfriend came over and made you promise not to tell; would it be tattling to tell me?* No, because someone older is trying to involve you in something he or she shouldn't be doing.

PREVENTING EMOTIONAL COERCION

Abusers may respond to a child's threat to tell in a variety of ways. If you make your children aware of these ploys before anything happens, they will have less impact and your children will be less vulnerable to abuse.

Bribery

What if the person who is bugging you says, "Oh, I'm sorry, I didn't mean to upset you, let's go get some ice cream and cake?"
That's bribery. We tend not to talk about bribery with children, perhaps because we use it. But your children need to know that the harder someone tries to get them to keep quiet about something, the more important it is to tell about it.

I Don't Care

What if they say, "Go ahead and tell, I don't care?" Children tend to believe that if that person doesn't care, no one will care. They need to know that you do care about what happens to them and they should come and tell you about what happened.

No One Will Believe You

What if they say, "Go ahead and tell, no one will believe you?" Children tend to think this anyway. Your children should know that any time they're not believed or not listened to, they should find someone else who will listen and who will help them.

Threats

What if they say, "If you tell, your mom and dad won't love you anymore" or *"If you tell, I'll do something to your dog or your baby brother or sister or your mom or dad,"* or *"I will hurt you or someone you care about if you tell."* The real message children need to hear from us is "This is a bigger problem than you can handle. No matter how scared you feel, you need to tell someone who can help you." Or for younger children: "That's not a real friend. You need to come and tell me about what happened so I can help take care of you. Don't be afraid to tell me. I'm a grown-up and I can help no matter what that other person says."

NO MORE SECRETS

The No More Secrets rule is an agreement you make with your family that you won't keep secrets anymore (not even in the family) and if asked to keep a secret, your children will say, "No, we don't keep secrets in our family and I'm going to tell." Younger children can simply say "No, I'm going to tell."

Surprises are okay. Surprises are things that make people happy that get told sooner or later, whereas secrets are never told. Children

quickly learn the difference, and by age four can respond to a request for secrecy about a birthday gift with "That's not a secret, it's a surprise."

Since 85 to 90 percent of perpetrators are known to the children, sexual abuse cannot take place without secrecy. Therefore, one of the first things a potential perpetrator will do is find out if the child can keep a secret. If a child steadfastly refuses, most abusers will not risk moving ahead.

CHILDREN AND SECRECY

Young children often confuse secrecy with whispering. Explain to them that telling something you only want one person to hear is different from keeping a secret. A secret is when they promise not to tell anyone else.

The No More Secrets rule does not say everyone must know everything. It says that your children will not agree to keep something in particular from anyone else in particular.

By age five or six, children can learn that there are many ways to be asked to keep a secret. They enjoy making a game of trying to trick Mom and Dad into keeping a secret without using the word secret. For example, what if someone says any of the following: "This is just between you and me." "Do you promise not to tell anyone else?" "You don't need to tell your mom and dad, I'll tell them later." "We won't tell them about our little game"? Your children should respond to all of these requests by saying "No, I don't keep secrets and I'm going to tell."

By age seven or eight, secrecy is such an integral part of children's lives with their friends that they are reluctant to give it up. This includes friendship clubs, secret bonds, oaths, pacts, etc. Essentially, we're allowing secrecy with peers and discouraging it with anyone older.

If a request for secrecy, whether or not the word secret is actually used, seems confusing or odd or compromising, one option open to older children is to say "I really don't like keeping secrets and I don't want to start now," or "I don't like this idea, let's do something else," or "I'd like to go home now."

Privacy is not the same as secrecy. Privacy means you can be by yourself or keep something to yourself. Secrecy means you're bound not to tell. Privacy respects individual needs. Secrecy creates shame in sexual abuse. It's important that children know the difference.

It is the *request* for secrecy that is important. Touching should never have to be a secret, and your children should tell any time someone tries to make touching a secret.

ADULTS HAVE RULES TOO

Children often get drawn into sexual abuse situations because they trust and love the abuser. They don't realize or understand that adults have rules too. One of those is: **Adults aren't allowed to ask children to do grown-up things.** The belief that adults are always in the right can interfere with a child's ability to listen to his or her own inner voice about a situation.

Children should know that adults have problems and that they make mistakes. Even if the adult says that an activity is okay, because they have a "special" relationship, children need to be prepared to say no and to tell someone about what happened. In fact, any time an adult asks a child to do something children don't usually do, he or she should say no and tell.

WHOM DO YOU TELL?

Your children should know that you want to hear about what is happening to them. We don't always listen very well and children don't always communicate very well, but they should know it's okay to keep trying until we understand what it is they want to say.

Telling should be like a reflex. Your children should feel that they can *always* tell you or someone else they trust what happened and they will be listened to. This reflex is instilled through previous experience and constant positive reinforcement. Each time we listen, we teach them that their feelings and questions are acceptable and will be taken seriously.

It is essential that you never tell your children whom they can trust. An abuser can be anyone. Children need to make their own decisions about who they trust. This was illustrated with one child who told me about her uncle. He had been abusing her for two years and she hadn't told anyone because her mother had said to her, "If anything ever happens to me, your uncle will take care of you. He loves all of us and you can always go to him with a problem." Since her uncle was the problem, the child didn't know what to do and she was sure her mother wouldn't believe her if she told.

Because children are afraid or ambivalent about telling, they often tell us in obscure ways that we don't understand. This is not necessarily anyone's fault, but it happens all the time. **For this reason, it is important to teach children to keep telling until someone hears them and helps with their problem.**

One of the common patterns in incest cases is that of a child who tells someone about the incest problem at about age six or seven. If that person doesn't listen or help, the child won't tell anyone else until about age twelve or thirteen, when he or she may run away rather than tell again.

WHO ELSE CAN YOU TELL?

Children need to know that adults have their own problems and worries, that they don't always listen well, and that sometimes they can't help. When this happens children need to know who else they can go to. For example, you might say to your children: "What if you had a problem and I was sick? Whom would you talk to?" "What if Dad wasn't very interested in listening because he was taking care of me, then whom could you tell?" "What if the next-door neighbor was out-of-town?" or "What if your teacher was grumpy that day and didn't have time to stop and talk?"

By asking them a series of questions, your children can begin to establish a list of people who care about them, who could help them. With problems as complex as sexual abuse, it is important to equip children ahead of time to get help when they can't talk to you. While adults can't prevent sexual abuse, children can if they are given permission to think for themselves, the ability to speak up for themselves, and the resources to get help when they need it.

CHAPTER 5
Identifying Strangers

Abduction and sexual abuse of children by strangers, although statistically less significant, so often ends in tragedy that our emphasis on teaching children how to deal with strangers is totally justified. How does it happen then that thousands and thousands of children each year go willingly with strangers? The answer lies in the disparity between what we say, what we mean, and what children hear.

In order to effectively shield our children from strangers who might abuse them, it is necessary to begin with some basic information about who these people are and how they behave. We need to understand what children believe about strangers and how that makes them more vulnerable. Finally, we need to balance the amount of supervision our children need with their ability to handle safely the freedom of movement they are given.

Who Are Stranger Offenders?

Stranger offenders (hereafter referred to as offenders) abuse children they don't know to fulfill their own needs for power and control. They see children as weak, helpless, defenseless victims who can easily be manipulated. They do not seek an intimate relationship with the child as do abusers who are known to the child. Instead they see children as objects for their use.

These offenders range from the passive exhibitionist to the sadistic murderer. Most of the violence against children during sexual abuse and abduction occurs with this group. Like the abusers who are known to the child, the stranger offender most probably was also abused as a child and directs the effects of his or her own abuse at children.

They are particularly adept at seducing children. Bribery, flattery, treats, and requests for help are common tricks. *While some strangers will literally snatch a child away, this happens less often than many believe because it is unnecessary and may attract attention. Most children who are abducted are lured into a seemingly innocent situation with someone who acts like a "nice" person. They go willingly, and, when they realize their mistake, it is often too late.*

Because there is no way to anticipate who these offenders are or what they will do, the best defense is to keep children away from strangers when they are unsupervised or in an isolated situation.

STRANGERS—THE CHILD'S POINT OF VIEW

Children have a pretty distorted sense of who and what strangers are. What we've said about strangers makes sense to *us*, but it doesn't always make sense to our children.

What is a stranger?

someone who tries to give you poison candy.

Someone who tries to make you get into a car.

Someone who wears a mask and has a gun in one hand and a knife in his pocket!

We've traditionally taught our children that the world is divided into two kinds of people—good guys and bad guys—and that the ones they need to worry about and watch out for are the bad guys. Of course, acting on this assumption is as impossible for children as it is for adults. The bad guys don't label themselves for us! Such an over-simplified definition is also dangerous because children—and adults—are consistently wrong, and often get hurt when they apply the safety rules from that point of view.

Teaching children to be afraid of bad strangers not only doesn't work very well, it is frightening. When we say things like "Don't talk to strangers or get in their car because they might take you away and we'd never see you again," we place a great burden on children. Instead of using fear tactics, you can give your children specific guidelines and information. This will limit their vulnerability while maintaining their ability to move freely in their everyday lives.

WHAT BAD GUYS LOOK LIKE

Young children see strangers as people who want to hurt little kids, who will try to lead them into dangerous situations, and who can be recognized because they look bad. From a child's point of view, staying safe is simply a matter of watching out for those people who look like their idea of a stereotypical stranger. Therefore, everyone else is okay. And yet we know that isn't true.

Someone who wants to hurt little kids.

Someone who tries to steal your dog and then get you to follow her.

Someone you don't know who wants to kidnap you!

I especially remember one child who said "A stranger is someone who wears a Band-Aid on his head." When I questioned him, he explained that his mother had said strangers hurt children because "they're a little bit sick up here," pointing to his head. Most of what we've said to children about strangers is vastly distorted and misunderstood. The good guys, bad guys notion gets translated into stranger = bad, so if someone isn't identifiably bad, children think he or she is not a stranger.

All discussions of strangers need to begin with: **A stranger is anyone you don't know.**

Even older children are confused about this. When you ask them what they think a stranger is, their first response is usually "Someone you don't know." When you ask them what a bad guy looks like, however, you get stereotypical answers such as "They're dirty, with messed up hair and an old car," "They have long fingernails and torn shoes," or "They're kind of sleazy-looking with shifty eyes."

The real danger to our children lies in their belief that "good" guys are easily distinguished from "bad" guys by appearance alone. As adults, we know that strangers who are dangerous can often be very kind, solicitous, and friendly. The problem is we really haven't expressed this to our children in a way they can understand.

How Do You Tell?

If we recognize that visual cues don't tell us whom to trust, then what do you say to your young children about strangers? First, help them understand that there is no way to tell by the way people look how they really are on the inside. With younger children you might ask "Could you misbehave when you were all dressed up in your very best clothes?" Conversely, there are times they've gotten dressed up like really bad guys. "Are you bad on the inside because you're wearing a mean witch's costume on the outside?"

For older children, talk about stereotypes. They should know that judging someone by appearances alone can be misleading.

Goodness and badness are not visible traits. There is no way to judge someone by how they look. Children who believe they can tell the good guys from the bad guys by how they look are in danger.

So Now What Do You Do?

Children need to learn about strangers: not any one kind of stranger in particular, but strangers in general, so that they can assume some responsibility for their own safety without feeling afraid. This is what allows children to function with freedom and confidence in the world.

After saying that strangers are anyone your children don't know, follow up by telling your children that most strangers are good, kind, friendly people. In fact, every single one of their new friends, teachers, coaches, doctors, and so on was a stranger when the child first met him or her. Most of them turned out to be people your children could trust.

The world is full of people who want to be around children. Some of those people are genuinely nice people. Some aren't. To illustrate this, talk to your children about a grouchy neighbor or someone who seemed nice at first but turned out not to be. What we're saying to children now is: You can't tell nice people from not very nice people by how they look.

Preparing to Change the Rules

The rules I teach children regarding strangers are based on two simple ideas. The first is: **There is only one person who is with you all the time, who can be responsible for keeping you safe all the time. That person is you.**

Most children believe that grown-ups will keep them safe. Children do not realize, until they are well into first grade, that they really are on their own much of the time. It is important to their safety that even very young children understand that Mom, Dad, teacher, and even baby-sitter are not always there and that, when they aren't, children are responsible for following the rules in order to keep themselves safe.

When talking about this idea with very young children, it is easier for them to understand by asking questions such as:

"Who's the only person there when you're out on the playground all by yourself?"

"Who's the only person that's with you all the time?"

"Then, who's the only person who can take care of you and keep you safe when you're all by yourself?"

"That's right, you are. Mom and Dad and your teachers and friends and the police are here to help and to teach you. But you're the one who always has to pay attention and keep yourself safe."

The second idea: **When children are alone, it is their job to take care of themselves. It is not their job to take care of the adults in the world.** If adults need assistance, they need to get it from another adult, not from a child.

One of the primary ways children get hurt by strangers is by being friendly and helpful. If they understand that taking care of themselves is their first priority when they're alone, they can comfortably ignore or deny adult requests for assistance.

STRANGERS—THE PARENTS' POINT OF VIEW

While we are rethinking what we say to our children about strangers, it is also important to look at how our own beliefs and feelings affect the decisions we make. Ambivalence about what we will do—not what we should do—sometimes crops up. For example, a friend of mine shared with me a situation that occurred at the end of a long afternoon of errands. She had taken her two preschoolers in and out of the car half a dozen times. Her youngest had finally gone to sleep, and she realized she had to run back into the market for something she had forgotten. She knew she shouldn't leave her children in the car, but she admitted thinking "It's only for a moment." Her better judgment prevailed, and despite the inconvenience, she once again took the children out of the car. But that feeling of being torn is completely natural. What matters is what we do when we feel torn.

These situations arise constantly:

► The phone rings and you run into the house to answer it, leaving your preschooler in the front yard.

► The washing machine goes off balance and you leave your toddler unattended to adjust it.

► Your first-grader has whined incessantly to be left in the toy section while you shop and you give in.

► Your kindergartner wants to walk to school alone and, against your better judgment, you agree.

Safety for you and your children is not just a set of rules. It's made up of lots of little decisions, some more obvious than others. It is important to recognize your ambivalence when it occurs. If you recognize it, you can *choose* what you will do rather than letting the situation or convenience choose for you.

PERSONAL SAFETY FOR CHILDREN

Personal safety for children has two distinct sides. **On the one hand there is the knowledge that your children are vulnerable no matter how careful you are. On the other is the recognition that children simply can't grow up if they aren't allowed, at some point, to move about in the world.** Personal safety involves teaching rules to your children so they know what to do when they're out on their own. It also includes making decisions about the limits you will set at various stages in your children's lives.

As obvious as this may seem, parents make decisions every day that fail to take into account the reality of the situations in which they place their children. If you don't know enough about your own decision-making process, it's hard to guide your children in learning to make their own sound decisions.

For example, I had several discussions with a mother whose kindergartner was very independent and demanded to walk to school alone. She could simply have said no, but she wanted to encourage his independence. After some discussion she gave him a choice. He could either walk with his mother until they could see the school and then she would watch while he walked the rest of the way alone or she would arrange for him to walk with an older child whose judgment she trusted.

Part of growing up for children is gradually being given the permission and the ability to do things on their own. Letting children know that they are indeed responsible for their own well-being when they're alone assures them that they can make decisions when they need to. Knowing that you will back them up on these decisions is fundamental to their safety, particularly as they get older and become subject to the pressures of being preteens.

That is not to say that children are responsible for raising themselves. Adults obviously bear the major responsibility for decisions about the care of children. However, **when children are alone, they, and only they, can make the necessary decisions to keep themselves safe.**

EXPANDING PRIVILEGES

Many times it is necessary and appropriate to take risks. Children have to do countless things for the first time in order to grow up. The key to making these kinds of decisions lies in understanding your own feelings about your child's request and in evaluating his or her maturity. A child can be very verbal and mature acting, but have demonstrated poor judgment in the past. Your decision must take all the factors into consideration.

Sometimes you'll let your children do something only to discover it was a mistake. For example, I recall a child who asked to stay and watch a street performer while her father shopped. He decided she was old enough to do so. When he returned, he saw his daughter sitting at an outdoor cafe table sharing an ice-cream cone with a woman he didn't know. At that moment, he had to quickly sort out the difference between what he was feeling and the actual situation. He told me he was filled with terror for what *might* have happened. At the same time, he knew he could use the incident as an opportunity to talk about what happened and to reestablish the rules with her.

In a similar situation, you should find out what your child thinks and believes about what happened. As a part of this discussion you may want to say something like "I understand that you thought it would be okay to talk to that person, she seemed nice enough. But when you are alone, you have to follow the rules." Your reaction should not make your child feel bad; it should be instructive and leave room for a future time when it will again be possible to honor his or her request to be left outside while you shop. Use the What If game to discuss other possible situations and to further clarify your expectations.

In order to learn to get along on their own, it is necessary for children to have opportunities to demonstrate that they can follow the rules. Let your children know what you expect. When children know you are counting on them, it is easier for them to live up to what is expected of them.

Establishing a Common Ground

I'm going to suggest some new rules and some changes in the old rules as we commonly know them. **In doing so, my first goal is to provide protection for your children by showing you how to teach clear concrete rules that prevent problem situations. The second is to help you help your children feel safe in the world. The important thing to remember is that children can be "smart" about their safety without being afraid.**

While the four rules outlined in the next chapter often seem stringent to adults, children naturally slot them in along with all the other rules in their lives, like brushing their teeth and making the bed. In teaching these rules to thousands of children, I've consistently found that they are glad to have clearly defined rules about strangers. They then know what is expected of them in a wide range of situations and they feel safer. You'll also feel more secure knowing that your children know what to do.

CHAPTER 6
Preventing Abuse and Abduction by Strangers

In order to protect your children, the rules they learn about strangers must be simple, straightforward, and practical. The following rules tell children *exactly* what to do in a wide variety of situations. They also provide guidelines for situations that are unpredictable. It is important that they be taught without creating fear or anxiety or suggesting that anyone wants to hurt your children.

Tell your children:

A stranger is anyone you don't know. There are four rules to follow when you're by yourself.

1. Stay an arm's reach plus away from strangers.

2. Don't talk to strangers.

3. Don't take anything from strangers, even something of your own.

4. Don't go anywhere with strangers.

Rule 1—The Arm's Reach Plus Rule

The first thing we have to do to maximize the safety of our children when they are not in the presence of a caretaking adult is to teach them to stay an *arm's reach plus* away from people they don't know even if they have to back up to do it. Teaching this rule is accomplished by playing the Stand Up, Back Up, and Run To . . . game, which shows how they can keep an eye on the stranger and also remain mobile. We are not teaching them to "run away." We want them always to run *to* a source of assistance, not to run without thought of where they could get help.

An arm's reach plus is: the length of an adult's arm plus the distance added when the adult bends over, plus a little bit more. Whenever a child is less than an arm's reach plus away from someone they don't know they should back up. The reason children need to stay at this distance is *not* because the person might want to hurt them, but because they want to keep themselves safe, and the best way to do that is to stay out of reach. Staying at a distance gives them the measure of safety they need if they feel uncomfortable about any situation and want to get out of it. This precaution also signals to an offender that this child is not an easy target.

Three- to Six-year-olds

For children as young as three and as old as six or seven, the stranger training game begins by teaching your children, as illustrated on the next page, what an arm's reach plus is.

Once your children understand how far away you want them to be, you can begin to illustrate the rule's use by acting out What If questions. This is accomplished through role-playing, by walking through the story and guiding your children as you go along. *This rule is difficult for children to picture when it's just described, so you actually have to demonstrate and practice it.* This role-playing should always be done in a relaxed way, without instilling fear. Be sure to explain through the entire game the idea that this person you're pretending to be is probably a nice person, but since your children can't tell by appearance alone, they have to follow the rules to stay safe.

"What if you were playing in the front yard and someone you didn't know—a stranger—came into the yard, I'd want you to stay an arm's reach plus away from that person. They might be a friend of Mom's or Dad's who you don't know. They might be anybody. But what I want you to do is pay attention and stay an arm's reach plus away. Could you do that? Let's pretend. I'll be the stranger. . . ."

The process of teaching the Stand Up, Back Up, and Run To . . . game is illustrated here. Begin by saying to your child,

"Okay, now Dad will be the stranger. What if you were playing in the sandbox and a stranger came into the yard? I want you to stand up as soon as you see that it's someone you don't know. I want you to pay attention and back up if the person comes close to you."

"That's right, you'd back up. There's nothing to be afraid of. You'd just pay attention and stay an arm's reach plus away. And you could back up again if the person took another step, couldn't you? Very good!"

The final step in teaching the Stand Up, Back Up and Run To . . . game is to say,

"What if the stranger kept moving toward you or you started to get nervous or scared, I'd want you to back up four more steps and turn and run into the house as quickly as you could. And I'd want you to yell really loudly so Mom or Dad would know you're coming and that you need us. Could you do that every single time you feel even a little bit scared? Good!"

Seven- to Twelve-year-olds

The arm's reach plus rule is no less valuable for seven- to twelve-year-olds, but the presentation is a little different.

By this age, children generally know that the way to stay safe is to maintain their distance from strangers. Having made clear the idea that there really isn't any way to tell the good guys from the bad guys by appearance alone, follow up with an introduction of the arm's reach plus rule along these lines:

"What if you were someplace where there weren't a lot of people around, like a field or playground, and you saw someone walking toward you. Do you think it would be smart to stay far enough away from that person so that you could get out of there if you began to feel weird about what was happening?"

"The arm's reach plus rule probably sounds babyish, but it's a good rule to remember. You always want to be able to get out of a situation that's making you uncomfortable, and if you keep your distance you'll be able to do that."

As they get older, embarrassment is a primary hindrance to children's ability to make decisions and take steps to keep themselves safe. They are much more aware of "how things look" and will often hesitate to follow their instincts because they feel it would be awful if they were wrong and the stranger turned out to be a "really nice person."

It's important to talk about this potential embarrassment with your children and to share some experiences you've had as an adult when you failed to keep yourself safe because you were reluctant to appear silly. Failing to cross the street when you feel you're being followed is one example. You may even want to ask older children outright, "Would it be embarrassing to keep backing up or to cross the street if a stranger was approaching you? I think it might be. But perhaps we sometimes have to choose between being embarrassed and being safe. I know I'd rather have you be safe."

RULE 2—DON'T TALK TO STRANGERS

This rule is an old one. It seems obvious and yet, for most children, if I walked into the yard and said, "Hi, my name's Sherryll, what's yours?" they would immediately answer me. The reason is very simple—that we teach our children to be polite. We often, without thinking, ask them to say hello to total strangers. As a result, **children think it is more important to be polite than to be safe.**

In order to change this, you must give your children specific permission to be rude—that is, to not respond—to a friendly "hello" of a stranger. Make clear to them that this rule applies when they are alone or with their friends, not when they are with an adult.

In fact, it is actually quite helpful for your children to talk to strangers when you are present. It is an opportunity for you to observe them, to teach appropriate behavior with adults and to later discuss your children's comfort or discomfort with the various people they meet.

If your children are hesitant to talk to a stranger, even if that stranger is a good friend of yours, you should support them. Let your children know that you trust their instincts and personal preferences.

BUT THEY KNEW MY NAME . . .

How many times have we seen children instantly perk up at the sound of their own name? They are completely disarmed, and make the entirely understandable assumption that someone knows them if he or she knows their name. How often I have heard children say, "He wasn't a stranger, he knew my name and he told me his name"?

Unfortunately, children can be too easily tricked into giving their names. One offender regularly started with "Hi, Larry," to which children responded, "I'm not Larry, I'm _____." From there he had a basis for conversation, and when the children later recalled what happened, they all thought he had known their names.

Talk with your children about some of the ways a stranger could have learned their names but not really know them. For instance, this might include reading it from their shirt, belt, books, or bicycle tag, or overhearing one of their friends, teachers, or parents call them by name. *If children hesitate to follow the rules because they are called by name, their level of safety decreases sharply. We must make it clear to them that knowing someone is more than exchanging names.*

You can help solve this particular problem by avoiding the use of clothing, barrettes, lunch boxes, and so on with your children's name displayed on them. Label their clothing and other possessions where the name will not be visible. If you already have items of clothing with your children's names displayed on them, save them for times when you are sure to be with them.

Talk to your children's teachers about the use of name tags on field trips. This practice coupled with the use of parent helpers the children may not know creates potential confusion. It makes it possible for strangers to pass themselves off as members of the group. One solution to this problem is to have children and leaders wear colored or shaped tags (bears, apples, birds). Anyone without a proper tag would be immediately recognized as separate from the group, and the children would know to seek the aid of someone with a tag like their own.

This is equally true for older children. To demonstrate this when teaching, I will often call a fifth- or sixth-grader, wearing his name on the back of his sports jersey, by name all the way through class. At the end of the class, I always ask if he knows how I knew his name. I cannot remember a time when the answer wasn't "Oh, I figured you knew my mom and dad or something."

Older children think they are less open to abuse and abduction. So do their parents. This is, at least in part, what makes them so vulnerable. As elementary as these rules seem, they are for children of all ages.

RULE 3—DON'T TAKE THINGS FROM STRANGERS, NOT EVEN YOUR OWN THINGS

While this rule also seems obvious, it is not. Children tend to think that it applies only to not taking treats like candy, toys, animals, and so on. They don't realize it can mean things like clothes or household objects. And they never foresee that it could include something they own and cherish. Once again, it is important to specify that this is a rule which applies *only* when children are not with a caretaking adult.

When children are with an adult and are offered candy, samples, or other treats, they should be taught to ask permission before taking it. When they are by themselves or with their friends, they must never take anything from someone they don't know.

Three- to Six-Year-Olds

To integrate the first three rules for example, say to your child, "What if someone you didn't know came up to you and said, 'Your dad left his keys at work and he wanted me to give them to you.' What would you do?" Actually acting this out, your child should stop what he or she is doing, stand up, back up, pay attention, not talk, and not take the keys. This sounds complex. It absolutely is not, even for preschoolers. All your children need is a clear statement of what you want them to do accompanied by a little practice.

Young children can be fooled by a familiar make-believe character. They should know that even dressed-up characters are not an exception to the stranger rules when they are by themselves.

I think my most poignant experience teaching this rule was when a five-year-old in one of my classes explained to me, "But what if someone said, 'Come here, little girl, and look at my bunnies.' I wouldn't, but what if they were just peeking up out of the box a little

bit and all I could see were their little eyes and ears and paws, and they looked so cute? It would be really, really hard, wouldn't it?" Children understand that following the rules isn't always easy.

Favorite Toys

There is one special What If game to role-play with your preschoolers. Pretend to be a stranger who walks into the yard, picks up one of your child's favorite toys, and tries to hand it to him or her. This is probably the most difficult game I play with children. They visibly teeter back and forth because they want their toy but they also want to follow the rule. I always acknowledge how hard it is for children not to take something that belongs to them, but it's part of the rule—children don't take anything from strangers.

When you play this What If game, tell your child you know how hard it is, but that he or she is more important than the toy. One effective way to say this is "If something happened to your doll, could we go to the store and buy a new one? Sure we could. If something happened to you, could we go to the store and buy another you? Of course not, that's silly. So as much as you love your doll, you're more important than she is. Mom and Dad love you more." Once children understand this, it is easier for them not to accept a favorite toy when it is offered by a stranger, but to come and tell you instead.

Seven- to Twelve-year olds

Seven- to twelve-year-olds also need to follow this rule. Practice by saying: "What if you were in the yard and a lady walked up with a book in her hand. She says she's a friend of your mom's and needs to get this book to her by tonight. Do you take it?"

The answer is no, because children do not take things from people they don't know, not even to be helpful. Most children tell me that the reason they don't take the book is because it might have poison ink! What a telling sign of how distorted children's perceptions of who strangers are, even for upper elementary age children.

There are two reasons you can provide your children for not taking things from people they don't know.

▶ It is their responsibility to take care of themselves, not adults, when they're alone or with their friends.

▶ There is no way to take something from a stranger and stay an arm's reach plus away.

Remind your children that is not their responsibility to take care of your book or any of your things. The adult can leave it on the porch, put it in the mailbox, or make other arrangements. This may seem overly cautious, but most children who get hurt by strangers are drawn in by apparently reasonable and harmless requests. *We cannot ask our children to judge situations involving strangers by the rationality of the request any more than by the appearance of the stranger, so they must have firm rules to fall back on.*

An excellent What If question for older children that explores the range of difficulties they might encounter would be "What if you're working on your bike in the park. Someone approaches you to look at it. When you back away, he steals your bike. What do you do? Would you be afraid to come home and tell us?"

Most of the What If questions I use come from actual stories children have told me. In this case, a professional associate described the day his son came home with a black eye and numerous cuts and bruises. Someone had stolen his bicycle. When his parents asked why he hadn't just let the person have it, he replied, "Because I knew you'd be mad if I didn't at least try to get it back."

Children should be very clear that you value them more than their possessions. Most children will sacrifice themselves for their toys, at least in part because they're afraid they'll get in trouble if they come home without them.

Rule 4—Don't Go Anywhere with a Stranger

Most children know not to go anywhere with a stranger. That's why strangers make up such good stories.

In both cases, the rule is clear. If Mom or Dad haven't said ahead of time that it's okay to go, don't go.

Perhaps because it's so painful to seriously consider the possibility of abduction, parents have a difficult time thinking of What If examples for this rule. Here are a few more:

"What if someone you don't know came and said your dog had been hurt and you had to come right away?"

"What if a stranger showed up at the basketball game and said I'd had a flat tire and he was supposed to take you to the gas station to meet me?"

"What if a neighbor, or someone else you know, came and said I'd told her to pick you up, but I hadn't said anything to you about it? Would you go?"

It is important that your children know in advance what they can expect from you and what you expect from them. Otherwise they take too much time to consider what the stranger is saying. This is time during which they could be in extreme danger. Instead, they need to be able to recognize immediately that this is not part of the rules their family agreed on and go for help.

THE CODE WORD

The code word is an agreement that you make with your children, six and up, that says: "If I ever send someone other than whom I said I would send to pick you up, he or she will know the code word. If the person doesn't know the code word, don't ever go with him or her, no matter what the person tells you." The code word can be anything, a word or even a sentence.

Children love using the code word. It neutralizes any anxiety and uncertainty they may feel about going or not going with a stranger in a particular situation. The code word easily and safely puts your children in charge of the situation. Once a code word has been introduced, children may want to change it. That's fine. There is no limit to the number of code words. Allow your children to use and change it as they need to, as long as everyone always knows what the current code word is.

Parents are sometimes careless about messages. For example, when you call your child's school and leave a message that is passed along by the sixth-grade monitor to the teacher, and from the teacher to your child, a margin of error is introduced. Whenever possible, give your messages directly to your children or use the code word. Permission via someone else should not be considered valid permission except in certain clearly defined cases. Your children should always get permission from the source—you.

For children who may be at higher risk for abduction (as in some custody cases), a code word can be established that is also known by specific individuals at the school. In this case, the child would never be released except to someone having the code word. I strongly recommend that you test this system before relying on it, as some schools are lax about enforcing such an agreement.

FEELING FUNNY INSIDE

Above and beyond all the rules, especially for older children, instinct, "that funny feeling inside," is their most important friend. Once children are in a dangerous or compromised situation, instinct must guide their decisions about how to survive.

Children talk about instinct in lots of ways, and the word is difficult to define, even for adults. For children's purposes, instinct is most simply defined as: **Instinct is nature's way of talking to you and helping to keep you safe.** Basically, whatever description children give for their own instincts is fine. The important factor is that with your encouragement they recognize their instinct as a legitimate tool so they can "listen" to and trust themselves.

RELAXING THE RULES

As children get older, they can gradually relax some of the rules. For example, by age seven and eight, children are beginning to feel they can say "hello" in response to a casual greeting on the street.

They should be able to do so and still understand that it is *not* okay for that "hello" to turn into a conversation or a question-and-answer session.

By age nine or ten, children may be allowed to answer a request for directions from someone in a car, if and only if they remain at least ten feet away from the car and are able to answer the question by a simple instruction. If the person asks them to look at an address, draw a map, or do anything requiring them to come closer, they need to tell the stranger to find someone else to help.

It is important to point out that just because a child begins to offer help doesn't mean that he or she can't stop *at any point* if they feel uncomfortable. This may seem rude and, perhaps, irrational. Nevertheless, children need to trust their own instinct and do whatever *they* feel they need to do for their own safety.

WHAT IF THEY GET ME ANYWAY?

At some point, children will ask, "What if they get me anyway?" This possibility *should not* be discussed until it is asked. At that point, talk about how their instincts might be useful to them. Help them to understand that it is *impossible* to create a rule for what they should do. Only their understanding of what is happening and their assessment of what they should do can guide them in that situation.

If they feel at that moment that they should kick and scream and do anything in their power to get away, then that is exactly what they should do. If their instinct tells them to be quiet and compliant and look for a chance to sneak away or wait to be let go, that is also exactly what they should do.

Talk about how they might get in touch with you. Be certain your children know where they live, what their full address and phone number are, and how to dial long distance. Be sure they know you would always want to know where they were, no matter what someone said to the contrary.

It should be stressed that all children need this information, but the specific subject of their options in the event of abduction is open for discussion only when your children bring it up. Prior to that time, you should teach the applicable rules and strategies only in the context of less fearful possibilities.

STRANGER RULES

► For children, a stranger is anyone they don't know.

► Children cannot tell the good guys from the bad guys.

► Children are the only ones who can be responsible for keeping themselves safe all the time.

► Children are responsible for taking care of themselves, not for taking care of adults. Adults who need assistance should go to another adult.

► Instinct is nature's way of talking to children—they should listen to that inner voice.

The four stranger rules for children to follow at all times when they are not with a caretaking adult are:

► Stay an arm's reach plus away from strangers.

► Don't talk to strangers.

► Don't take anything from strangers, not even your own things.

► Don't go anywhere with a stranger.

CHILDREN PREVENT ABUSE AND ABDUCTION

As with sexual abuse by people known to the child, there are limits to the precautions parents can take to protect their children from abuse and abduction by strangers. Strangers approach children when they are alone or with a group of friends. For that reason, your children must be prepared to take care of themselves when they're not with you.

The decisions you make regarding increasing your children's freedom should be based on what you know about their ability to follow the rules and your assessment of their maturity. But you don't do it alone. Protecting children from abuse and abduction by strangers is a partnership between you and your children. If you teach your children about strangers as positively and clearly as you teach them to cross the street, they will not only have a healthier attitude about the world, they will also be safer.

CHAPTER 7

Staying Alone

Leaving children to care for themselves is a controversial issue. I will not make a case for or against it. The Children's Defense Fund of Washington DC estimates that 5.2 million children age thirteen and under are regularly left to supervise themselves, generally before or after school, or both. The simple fact is that children are left alone and we need to make them as safe as possible.

Even if you think you *never* leave your children alone, there are times when you do: You're in the shower and someone comes to the door; or you're in the garden and the phone rings. With only the rarest exceptions, all children are alone—however briefly—at one time or another and they wonder and worry about what could happen at those times. Knowing your children's concerns and discussing them using the What If game not only reassures them, but it prepares them to be safer.

GROUND RULES

Children, like adults, do better when they know what is expected of them. That is why it is so important to have established ground rules. The What If game is a natural way to go over the wide range of things that could come up when your children are by themselves.

Using the game you can set limits regarding a variety of issues that may arise.

The following checklist, which you can make copies of, is a helpful guide to use in making sure your children know their name, address, and phone number. Use it also to give them emergency numbers, to make sure they know how to make telephone calls, to establish basic rules, and to set expectations.

Command of the items on this checklist will ensure that your children understand the essential ground rules for spending time alone. Review it often, even if their time alone consists only of your momentary, unplanned absences.

STAYING ALONE CHECKLIST

My name _____

My parents' names _____

My address _____

My phone number _____

My parents' work phone numbers _____

_____

Police _____

Fire _____

Doctor _____

Resource people _____

_____

_____

Neighbors _____

_____

Other _____

If the phone rings I will _____

_____

If someone comes to the door I will _____

_____

I can let the following people in _____

_____

If there is an emergency _____

_____

If I get scared _____

_____

If I get bored _____

_____

My responsibilities are _____

_____

_____

_____

NEGOTIATING GROUND RULES

If you decide to let your children stay alone, you have to determine what limits to set. Your children will press for more freedom while you will generally try to hold the line for the sake of safety and structure on such issues as: when to be home, how far from home to go, whether they can have friends in, what snacks they can have, when to do their homework, what TV to watch and so on. This process of negotiating the limits can provide an important opportunity to discuss safety and personal responsibility.

I use a simple chart to list the privilege desired on one side and the associated responsibilities on the other. Children are amazingly good at coming up with the responsibilities associated with a privilege. They can often articulate your concerns better than you can.

For example, children often want to be able to have friends in when they stay alone. In this situation, and many, many others as children get older, the following rights and responsibilities exercise can be very useful. It allows both of you to look carefully at the privileges your children want, the responsibilities that go with them, and to agree on the limits.

PRIVILEGES

1. I want to be able to have a friend over after school, even if there's no adult here.

RESPONSIBILITIES

1. We won't talk on the phone too long.
2. We won't go outside the yard.
3. We'll watch little brother.
4. We'll do our homework.

Once the chart is complete, discuss it. If your children feel they are up to the responsibilities, you can grant them the privilege for a test period. *The beauty of this approach is that children will sometimes look at the list and decide they don't want, or can't handle, the privilege just yet.* Another benefit is that when children are unable to meet the responsibilities, the privilege is withdrawn, and the children—not you—are responsible for the loss of the privilege.

One of my favorite applications of this exercise is with preadolescent girls who want a horse. After detailing all the responsibilities that go with a horse, including the expense, they are usually able to say that they still want a horse *and* that they can see how impossible it is for them to take on that responsibility.

ANSWERING THE TELEPHONE

I find that parents frequently think their children know how to use the telephone when they don't. Take the opportunity as you work through the following rules to actually have your children demonstrate that they can use the telephone. If you have an autodialer, put pictures of people next to the numbers so your young children can call quickly and easily in an emergency. Older children should understand how to use each telephone in the house.

Your children must know to *always* answer the phone when they are home alone. First, it is your line of communication with them. Second, it is frightening for children to sit and listen to the phone ring and ring, not knowing who it might be. Finally, burglers often call first to find out if anyone's home.

SAFE TELEPHONE PROCEDURES FOR GENERAL CALLS

▶ Answer the phone, with "Hello," not with a first or last name, such as "This is Lisa" or "Williams residence." Children should not give their name out or answer any questions over the phone unless they are talking to a family member or close family friend.

▶ They should then say, "My mom is busy, may I take a message?" or "My dad is lying down, may I take a message?"

▶ If the caller doesn't comply with this, children should say again, "May I take a message?"

▶ If the caller still refuses, children should hang up the phone. This is not rude. The telephone is for communicating, not playing games.

▶ If your children cannot take messages, for whatever reason, they can ask the caller to call back at a specified time.

SPECIAL CALLS

Prank calls. Whether they are silly ("Have you got Prince Albert in a can?") or threatening ("I'm following you."), children should hang up immediately. Prank callers need a response in order to "play their game." When they don't get it, they usually stop.

Repeated prank calls. Whether they are being made by children or adults, whether they are silly or threatening, if someone keeps calling and calling, especially if it's frightening, children should call a parent or an adult friend to help.

Sales calls. It is all right for children to interrupt and say "No, thank you," then hang up the phone. It is not rude for children to interrupt if the person calling is long-winded.

Survey calls. Children should know to say "No, thank you" and hang up the phone, even if the caller offers a free prize or money to children if they answer their questions.

Question calls. Children should understand not to answer anyone's questions over the phone. Even if the caller says they must answer their questions, it is not true. Children should know that no one has to answer questions over the phone. It is all right for them to say "No, thank you" and hang up.

"I'm watching you" calls. If you think about it, most children come home from school, go to the kitchen to make a snack, and turn on the television. So someone who calls and says "I can see you, you're in the kitchen making a snack, now do everything I say" is making a pretty safe guess about any child after school and is probably a harmless prankster. As with any other prank call, the thing to do is hang up. If children feel frightened in this or any other situation, they should have the name of *someone to call.*

The key to safety with all telephone calls is to impress upon your children that they are in control. Hanging up is always an acceptable way to handle a problem caller.

ANSWERING THE DOOR

Children must also know to always go to the door when they are home alone and answer it, but not open it. Children who pretend they're not home feel frightened and powerless. They are also in danger because burglars usually knock first and will not enter a home that is occupied. The key to remember here is that children *do not open* the door for *anyone* except a member of the family or a friend if they have permission.

When children are home alone, they are responsible first and foremost for themselves. They do not need to be helpful to someone who comes to the door. It is important that your children are comfortable saying no, even to someone with a good story.

SAFE DOOR PROCEDURES

Children who are home alone should:
► Always keep the house locked.
► Always go to the door when someone knocks.

▶ Ask "Who is it?"

▶ Not open the door for anyone except a member of the family or a friend, if they have permission.

Some Specific Examples

▶ If the person asks for their parents, children should say "My mother is in the shower" or "My father is on the telephone."

▶ If the person has a delivery, children should have the delivery left outside.

▶ If the delivery requires a signature, children can send the person to a neighbor or have him or her come back later.

▶ If there has been an accident, an emergency, or just a flat tire, and someone wants to use the phone, children should not open the door. They can get the information and make the call for the person.

BEING SCARED: FEAR VERSUS BEING SPOOKED

There is a significant difference between being really frightened and feeling increasingly nervous and jumpy when you're home alone. Ask your children what frightens them. Talk about how it feels to be spooked versus how it feels to be really afraid. Decide with them whom it would be okay to call when they're just nervous about hearing noises and whom they should call when it's a real emergency.

KNOWING NORMAL NOISES

This is an enjoyable and easy exercise that actually identifies the noises that are always around but that we don't hear until we begin feeling a little scared. To do this exercise, sit down with your children and listen very carefully to the noises in and outside the house. Write down all the noises you hear: the refrigerator motor, the heating system, a branch scraping on the window, snow shifting on the roof, whatever. This exercise should be repeated from time to time because household noises change at different times of the year and even different times of the day. When children know what the normal noises are, they won't get spooked so easily.

EMERGENCIES

Although we pay lip service to emergency preparedness, most families don't even have an emergency escape route for fires. Most parents don't discuss how to get out of the house if a burglar should enter. Most families don't have basic first aid supplies or training. Since the three most common emergency situations are fires, robberies, and accidents, this lack of preparation creates a life-threatening situation for children who stay alone.

I've had many revealing conversations with children about how they propose to handle basic emergencies. Their ideas can be very distorted. Following are some common responses to What If questions:

This is only one of the frightening examples of how literally our children take what we say to them. It strikingly points out the need to structure personal safety training so children learn to think about the situations they're in rather than blindly following the rules that apply to "safe" situations.

Children need to know what is expected in an emergency, whom to call, and how to make an emergency call. They need to know that all the rules are called off in a life-threatening situation and that they have your permission to do whatever needs to be done at that moment to protect themselves and each other.

RESOURCES FOR HELP

The single greatest factor for children who feel good about staying alone seems to be the availability of their parents and other resource people. Knowing this, parents and employers can work together to make it easy for children to check in. It establishes a link so children can let someone know they're all right. It also means they know they have someone to call if they're not.

Having the option to call makes a difference in how children feel about being alone. If it's not possible for children to call, parents should designate someone else who can take that call, someone who will take a few minutes to chat, someone who children will feel comfortable talking to about a problem.

STAYING ALONE SAFELY

Leaving your school-age children by themselves, even for short periods of time, is a very personal choice. It can be a nurturing, satisfying, and safe experience if it is planned, discussed, and monitored openly and conscientiously. *Children who have siblings staying with them, neighbors who are willing to be a resource, and predetermined guidelines about chores, homework, television, recreation, and so on do better than children who are genuinely "on their own."*

If you leave your children alone, don't feel guilty. Instead, put your energy into making it a safe and satisfying experience for everyone. Staying alone can be a very positive learning opportunity for many children.

CHAPTER 8

Making Exceptions to the Rules

Being told that your children are really well-behaved, polite, and considerate can be a delightful surprise and is a sign of how well they follow the rules when you are not around. Such praise seems positive, but it isn't in all situations. When children follow a common rule in an uncommon situation, the results can sometimes be tragic.

We try to encourage our children to think for themselves, but we rarely encourage them to evaluate rules and to make exceptions when they feel they need to. This is a cause for our concern because children who feel bound by everyday rules are often unable to get themselves out of problem situations.

In order for your children to know what to do when rules conflict, they must have your permission to make exception *to any rule*, if making that exception will keep them safe or allow them to get out of a dangerous situation.

A few examples:

▶ We teach our children to be polite, then we tell them not to talk to strangers. Which message is stronger when a friendly person walks into the yard and says "Hi"?—being polite or not talking to strangers?

▶ We encourage children to be helpful and we teach them not to take things from strangers. Someone from work drops by and asks your child to give you an important package. Your child doesn't know the person. Would it be okay with you if your child refused the package?

▶ We teach our children not to keep secrets, then we ask them to. How do children learn when exceptions are okay and when they are not?

▶ We teach our children the code word. Then we send someone to pick them up without giving them the code word. Will the children get in "trouble" if they refuse to go?

▶ We teach our children to "mind" without telling them that they don't have to if the request seems wrong.

▶ We teach our children not to lie, without recognizing that lying might be necessary to get them out of a dangerous or compromising situation.

▶ We teach children not to make too much noise in public places without saying they can "scream like crazy" if they need to.

▶ We tell them it's all right to hang up on pranksters. Do we then get upset if the prankster they hung up on was an old college friend?

▶ We tell them not to open the door or accept deliveries when they're home alone. What message do they get if we then grumble all the way to the post office to retrieve a special delivery letter?

Rules create structure and are crucial to stability, order, and routine in children's lives. While exceptions cannot be taught until rules are established, they are equally important. There are many times when children need to be able to make exceptions to the rules. Children who have discretion as well as responsibility for the rules are better able to keep themselves safe.

BEING POLITE

We teach our children to be polite. At the same time, it is important to help children develop the ability to judge and decide about being polite in any given situation. This is true for children of *all* ages. As they grow up, we want to give them permission to be rude or non-responsive when *they* feel they need to be. At the same time, we can teach them appropriate behavior. For example, if your child sticks his or her tongue out to express dislike, an instructive response might be "It's okay that you don't like her. You can let her know that by not talking to her or looking at her. You don't need to stick your tongue out for her to understand that you don't like her right now."

Knowing they have permission to be rude helps children say no to sexual abuse. It makes it easier for them to ignore or walk away from strangers. It helps them to feel less bound to please adults to their own detriment. One of the most frequent reports I hear from children who have been sexually abused is that they didn't want to hurt the person's feelings or appear rude.

LYING AND BREAKING PROMISES

Parents who teach that lying is totally unacceptable might be surprised to hear that their children are seriously compromised in their ability to keep themselves safe and to report abuse. For example, I've known children who were abused and the perpetrator refused to let them go unless they promised not to tell. These children kept their promises. It was not until their parents began to notice changes in their children, which they questioned, that their children revealed what had happened.

Children must know that it's okay to tell, even when they promised they wouldn't, if they were threatened or intimidated into promising. This is a difficult exception to teach prior to about age six. For children under six, a promise not to tell is the same as a secret and your children should know not to keep secrets, even if they said they would.

It is absolutely essential that your children be given the option of lying if they need to to keep themselves safe or to get out of a risky situation. You give them this permission with the specific agreement that when they need to tell a lie, they must also come and tell you as soon as possible that they needed to do so and why.

It is my experience that children do not abuse this right and that they will come home and tell, if they know you will support them and listen carefully to their story.

BLIND OBEDIENCE

We need to look at the ways in which we teach our children to be blindly obedient to adults and authority figures. Most children do not know they can say no to a police officer, a teacher, a principal, a counselor, a minister, a baby-sitter, or a parent when an inappropriate request is made.

Children need to know that they, and *they alone*, can and should be the judge of the appropriateness of any request. Because you cannot and should not always be available to make choices for your children, you must give them the ability to make choices for themselves.

Teaching this idea can be silly and fun and doesn't interfere with teaching children respect for adults. Use examples such as:

▶ *"What if your teacher said, 'For art today, we're all going to cut little tiny dots out of our shirts and paste them on a piece of paper.'?"*

Children will say, "Of course, I wouldn't do that. We don't cut holes in our clothes."

▶ *"What if the baby-sitter asked to take a bath with you?"*

Children often say, "I'd say no, the baby-sitter can take a bath when she gets home."

▶ *"What if a policeman asked you to hold his gun or drive his police car?"*

Children usually laugh at this and say, "I wouldn't do that, even if a policeman said to." Children should be told that a uniform does not mean they should do as they're told automatically. Even with a policeman, children should have permission to think about what they're being asked to do and say no.

Children already know that their parents and other grown-ups make mistakes sometimes. It is important to talk about what they should do if Mom or Dad or someone else in the family asks them to do something they know they shouldn't do. Saying no to someone in the family is as important as saying no to people outside the family.

▶ *"What if Dad said you could go across the street to get your ball, but there was a car coming?"*

Children who feel comfortable about Dad making a mistake can say, "I wouldn't go if there was a car coming, even if Dad said okay."

▶ *"What if Mom asked you to keep a secret?"*

If the person who made the rule breaks it, children should feel free to speak up. "Mom, you know we don't keep secrets."

▶ *"What if Mommy's boyfriend asked you to do something you knew was wrong and you were scared to say no because Mommy likes him?"*

Children are at greater risk for abuse with boyfriends and new stepfathers. Prepare your children by letting them know they can say no whenever they need to, that you will believe them and that you won't be mad.

The central message underlying all of these stories is this: There isn't anyone in the entire world that your children can't say no to, if they are asked to do something they think is wrong, that could hurt them, or that they know you wouldn't want them to do.

You need to talk with your children about rules, exceptions, and expectations that allow them and you to trust one another. Use specific examples and What If questions until you're confident they know the difference between blindly doing what they're told and saying no when they need to.

CHAPTER 9
Choosing Child Care

As the percentage of two-income and single-parent families continues to rise, the need for quality child care has become acute. Leaving
your children in someone else's care is, as you well know, one of the
most critical decisions you make. Yet most parents know very little
about how to choose and monitor this care.

While it is virtually impossible to remove all the risks, there are
guidelines that can help you reduce the vulnerability of your children
to abuse by caregivers. The lists I provide here should be added to
your overall considerations of any caregiver.

Child care generally falls into several categories:

▶ Licensed or unlicensed group day care includes any facility that
cares for children, whether it has an education program or not.

▶ Supervised or unsupervised family day care is care in
someone's home and often includes the caregiver's own
children. Supervision may be provided by a sponsoring referral
agency that matches children to specific homes.

► In-home and out-of-home individual care refers to people who provide care specifically for your children in your home or theirs.

► Finally, there are baby-sitters, who also need special guidelines to help prevent abuse.

While checklists can be useful, the most important guide you have is your own instinct, your gut reaction to the people and the place where you leave your children. No matter what the checklist says, if your instinct says no, go elsewhere.

LICENSED AND UNLICENSED GROUP DAY CARE

Any facility that cares for children, whether licensed or not, should meet stringent standards. These are in addition to any questions and concerns regarding location, cost, education, and other services.

CHECKLIST FOR LICENSED AND UNLICENSED CENTERS

The Facility

► Is the facility licensed? If not, why not?
► What is the general atmosphere?
► Is it clean?
► Are there separate bathroom facilities for children and adults?

The Staff

► Do they seem to enjoy the children? Are they actively interested in what the children are doing?
► How do they talk to the children? How much of what is said is corrective ("no," "stop it") versus instructive?
► Is the staff more interested in the children or in talking to you? Are they able to do both?
► What are the credentials of the staff?

► How long has each person been there?

► What are they paid?

► Whom do they use for substitutes? What are their credentials and how often are they used?

► Are staff members related to one another? If so, how? How long have they worked together? Check all their references.

► Do staff members indiscreetly complain about any particular children or families?

► Are there any other adults present whose purpose is not clear?

► Are there any relatives of staff members who hang around without apparent purpose?

Center Activities

► Are the children involved in their activities? Or do they appear to be looking for something to do?

► Is there a balance between planned activities and free time?

► Are you welcome to drop in at any time? This is extremely important. If not, why not?

► Is the children's work displayed? Is it current?

Supervision

▶ How is free time supervised?

▶ What is the adult-to-child ratio?

▶ Is the director always present? If not, who is reponsible?

▶ Are the children ever left with only one adult? If so, what happens in an emergency?

▶ How secure is the facility? Could someone come in and pick up a child unnoticed?

▶ Is the playground secure? Are there blind spots where children can't be seen?

▶ Is the playground open to the public?

▶ How are messages handled? Is this a secure system?

References

▶ Ask for professional references.

▶ Ask for a list of families whose children attend the center, and call them.

▶ Talk with them about the strengths and weaknesses of the center. Find out what problems or concerns they have had. How were they resolved?

Deciding

▶ Trust your instincts. If you're not comfortable with the facility, do not compromise and do not send your children there.

Monitoring

▶ Offer to help on periodic field trips.

▶ Drop in unexpectedly several times a year, including during nap time.

▶ Talk to your children about their day.

▶ Learn to follow up on their answers with additional questions that keep the conversation going. That's where you learn what really happened during their day.

▶ Ask questions like:
   What did you do today?
   Did anything special happen?
   Are there any new people at the school?
   Did you go anywhere special?
   What did you do at playtime?
   Did you take a nap?

▶ If your children tell you about something they didn't like or that made them feel bad, ask more questions like:
   What does Ms. _____ do?
   Did you tell her you didn't like it?
   What did she do or say next?
   How did you feel when she said that?
   Would you like me to help by talking to her?

Let your children know that you can help with problems at the school and demonstrate this by talking with the staff even if it's about a small problem. It shows your children that they can call on you for larger problems.

TAKING YOUR OWN CONCERNS SERIOUSLY

Immediately act on any hunches you have. Talk to other parents. Find out if they're having similar problems or concerns. Do not be swayed by easy answers or dismissal by any member of the center staff until you are satisfied with the answer.

Some examples:

▶ What if your child came home with someone else's underwear on and the center says he messed his pants and they borrowed someone else's second pair? Call the other parents.

▶ What if your child comes home with stars on his or her buttocks and upper thigh and the center says it's their way of positively reinforcing potty training? Ask your children what the stars are for.

▶ What if your child comes home with a story about riding to the airport in a van and the center staff says he or she is confused, they read a story about it? Children know the difference between what they do and what they read about. Ask some other parents.

▶ What if your children come home with stories about people taking pictures of them and the center staff says that's true and shows you pictures of classroom activities, but you don't feel that's the whole story? Ask other parents about what their children are saying.

All of these situations occurred at one preschool. In each case the director allayed the concerns of parents with logical explanations. It was only after one child revealed his own abuse and the parents got together that they learned that each of these questions had been a clue to their own children's abuse. Considering just isolated events, none of the parents were able to see what was happening.

Paranoia about day care does not prevent child abuse. Careful screening and close monitoring can very effectively protect children. The only child who was not abused at the center just referred to was the one whose mother worked flexible hours and could be expected to show up at any time.

SUPERVISED AND UNSUPERVISED FAMILY DAY CARE

This type of care includes all the people who take children into their home, usually added to their own small children, in a kind of group baby-sitting arrangement. In some cities this is supervised by a monitoring agency. In others it is completely unmonitored. Because this is a closed environment, you must be particularly careful when selecting this kind of care.

CHECKLIST FOR SUPERVISED AND UNSUPERVISED FAMILY DAY CARE

Initial Screening

▶ Do you know the person personally?
▶ If not, ask for references and the names of other parents whose children she cares for.
▶ Call the parents and ask about problems, things that annoyed or concerned them? How were they resolved?

Visiting the Home

▶ What is the general atmosphere?

▶ Is it clean?

▶ Who else lives in the home? Are these people ever there when the children are there?

▶ Is the house large enough to comfortably accommodate the number of children being cared for?

▶ Is the yard secure? For preschoolers, this is essential.

▶ Are the doors easily opened by a small child?

▶ Are there adequate toys and activities for the children?

▶ Does it look like children live and play there?

Get to Know the Caregiver

▶ Where are the children she is caring for? Where are her own children?

▶ Does she seem to enjoy the children?

▶ How does she talk to the children? How much of what is said is corrective or punitive versus instructive?

▶ What is the maximum number and ages of the children in the home?

▶ What is her education and experience?

▶ Check her past employers, if any.

▶ How does she relate to your children?

▶ Is she more interested in money, hours, and whether you'll ever be late than in your children's needs?

▶ Ask questions like:
How does she discipline?
What would she do with the children in an emergency?
Do the children play outside alone?
Do they nap? When? Where?
What television programs are the children allowed to watch?

▶ Is there an assistant? Ask all the same questions about the assistant.

▶ Are you welcome to drop in at any time?

Deciding

▶ Trust your instincts! If you have to sell yourself on this arrangement, find someone else.

Monitoring

▶ Talk to your children. Find out how they feel about being there. (See the Checklist for Licensed and Unlicensed Day Care.)

▶ Drop in unexpectedly from time to time. Change your child's scheduled pickup time every so often.

▶ Immediately act on any concerns you have. Talk to other parents. Do not put up with problems because it would be hard to find another arrangement.

IN-HOME AND OUT-OF-HOME INDIVIDUAL CARE

In selecting people to care for your children in your own home or in theirs, remember that the safety and well-being of your children is being granted to them. Be sure you know what their experience is. Thoroughly check their references and past employers. Notice how they relate to your children. Are they more interested in your children or their own working conditions? How do you feel about them? If you are not comfortable with one person, find someone else. This does not mean that you should hold out for the "perfect" person or that there won't be problems and adjustments. But you must begin with a comfortable base.

Be sure to set specific guidelines and expectations. Do you want someone to care for your children and clean house? Or do you want someone solely to care for your children? Since you are giving the care of your children over to someone else for a period of time, the more they know about your expectations and values about childrearing, the better job they can do.

BABY-SITTERS

As dire as the baby-sitter shortage may be, it is important to check your baby-sitters out. Who else do they sit for? Call those parents. Ask if they had any problems or if they still use that sitter.

Parents commonly leave their children with a baby-sitter and, as they're walking out the door, say, "Now, do everything the baby-sitter says." Think about the message implicit in that! It contradicts everything we've been discussing about a child's ability to be responsible and to exercise the skills we are teaching them. The fol-

lowing recommendations will increase the ability of children to keep themselves safe. It also may result in the loss of a baby-sitter or two. I'm sure you'll agree this is a difficult, but ultimately worthwhile tradeoff in order to protect your children.

When a baby-sitter comes to the house, go over the ground rules for the evening *in the presence of your children*. This includes what they eat, what TV shows and games are allowed, when they go to bed, whether they need a bath and if so, whether they need assistance, whether they need help getting ready for bed, whether they get snacks, and so on. When this information is covered in the presence of the children it takes away the baby-sitter's ability to say, "Your parents said . . . and you're really going to get into trouble if they find out you didn't do what I told you to."

Baby-sitters need to be told that you do not permit deviations from these guidelines and that your children will have been instructed to tell you if any are proposed. Tell them also that your children do not keep secrets and will tell you if they are asked to do so. It is important for parents to remember that, first and foremost, the job of a baby-sitter is the care of the children, not being a pal. If the baby-sitter is totally intimidated by these new ground rules, you should let him or her know that you're glad they're there, and it just makes you feel better to give your "standard baby-sitter speech."

Finally, in all child-care arrangements, as in all other situations, the best defense your children can have against sexual abuse is the prevention training you give them, your willingness to listen carefully to them, and your ability to ask questions about their concerns.

CHAPTER 10

When Children Are Sexually Abused

There is no way to anticipate or remove all the risks for our children. In spite of everything we do, some children will be sexually abused. If this happens in your family, another aspect of safety and protection begins—guiding your child through the process of recovery. This is an effort that may seem in conflict with your desire to put it all behind you, with the needs of the system to investigate, and with any attempt to prosecute.

HOW CHILDREN TELL US

As you've seen from previous examples, children often do not know how to tell us they have been sexually abused or that they have successfully resisted abuse, and don't know quite what to do next. There are numerous reasons for their hesitancy to talk about what has happened, including their relationship to the abuser, fear of the consequences, retaliation, or uncertainty about whether or not they will be believed.

This ambivalence can result in some pretty obscure attempts to tell what happened to them. For example, one little girl I know said to her father, "Uncle Smitty is ugly." When it was later revealed that she had been sexually abused by Uncle Smitty, her father asked why she hadn't told. She adamantly informed him that she *did* tell and cited the day she had said "Uncle Smitty is ugly." While it is important to teach children to say what they mean, it is equally necessary for parents to learn to listen for what they *mean*, as well as what they say.

More often than not, we discover sexual abuse by observing children's behavior.

Some of the signs you can be aware of include:

► Sudden reluctance to go somewhere or be with someone.

► Inappropriate displays of affection or explicit sexual acts.

► Sudden use of sexual terms or new names for body parts.

► Uncomfortableness or rejection of typical family affection.

► Sleep problems, including insomnia, nightmares, refusal to sleep alone, or sudden changes in habits such as insisting on having the light left on.

► Regressive behaviors, including thumb-sucking, bed-wetting, infantile behaviors, or other signs of dependency.

► Extreme clinginess or other signs of fearfulness.

► Depression and withdrawal.

► A sudden change in personality.

► Problems in school.

Any one of these signs could indicate sexual abuse, or it could be indicative of another problem. You should look into whatever problem may have precipitated such a change in your child's behavior. They are sure signals that he or she needs help.

HOW SHOULD WE RESPOND?

The trauma of children reporting sexual abuse is very real, and **one of the most important factors in a child's ability to recover is the reaction of the first person he or she tells.** The foremost concern at that moment should always be calm support.

When children report sexual abuse, they should immediately be told that:

1. **You believe them and you're glad they told.**

2. **They didn't do anything wrong.**

3. **The perpetrator shouldn't have done what he or she did.**

4. **You will do your best to see that they are not alone with that person again until the problem is resolved.**

Do not promise your child that you will do anything specific. You may not be able to meet that promise, and it will only add to your child's overall frustration, disappointment, and sense of betrayal.

Give yourself some time to think. Parents of abused children are themselves abused. They too feel guilt, rage, and a sense of loss. It is important to take care of yourself as well as your children.

If medical assistance is required immediately, a facility specializing in rape crisis intervention is preferable. Such facilities have the necessary training and materials. General anesthesia is usually not recommended to facilitate the examination. While it makes the physical process easier, it increases a child's sense of helplessness and loss of control.

Whatever medical treatment is required, children should be allowed to participate in the process so they don't feel further victimized by having things "done to them." Let them know where they'll be going. Tell them what will be done and why it is important. Simply saying "The doctor wants to check you and make sure everything is okay" is a good beginning.

Child sexual abuse is a specialized field. Not everyone is comfortable talking to children about what has happened to them. If your own physician is not familiar with child sexual abuse or doesn't feel comfortable discussing what has happened, ask for a referral to someone who is experienced, who knows what to look for and how to talk to children about what has happened to them.

The emotional damage children experience from sexual abuse is affected by many things. Recovery is enhanced when children know that they are believed, that they didn't do anything wrong, and that they will not be subject to further abuse. As a parent, you have an opportunity—and a responsibility—to protect your child's emotional well-being during and after the time the abuse is reported.

WHAT ABOUT REPORTING?

The decision to report sexual abuse is difficult, especially when the perpetrator is a friend, someone well-known in the community, or a member of the family. It is important, as you are considering whether or not to report, to remember that the *total* responsibility for the offense lies with the perpetrator. No parent is ever responsible for ruining an abuser's life by reporting.

Children need to participate in the decision to report whenever possible. Ask your child how he or she feels about reporting the abuser. I find that most children want the offender to get help *and* they want to protect other children from future abuse.

Your decision to report needs to include consideration of your child's safety and ability to recover. It also needs to include a consideration of other children. The average pedophile abuses dozens of children in his or her "career" of offending. Your child probably was not the first, nor will he or she be the last.

Many parents—motivated by outrage, disbelief, and a fear of falsely accusing—want to talk to the accused abuser before reporting. I strongly discourage this. Perpetrators are very convincing and will only confuse the situation by their denial. Call your local child protective services agency, social services, or police department. You do not need evidence or anything other than your child's story. The job of investigating belongs to the system.

If you wish to consult someone prior to reporting who can help you decide whether to report, it is important that you understand the Mandatory Reporting Law. In all fifty states and the District of Columbia, professionals (that is, anyone who works in a position of trust with children, including doctors, nurses, teachers, and social workers) are required by law to report all suspected cases of child abuse or neglect. This means that the professional you consult, with few exceptions, will be bound by law to report the case. Parents who are not aware of this law can be devastated by an unexpected police or social services investigation.

WHAT HAPPENS NEXT?

Once a decision to report is made, parents need to retain as much control of the process as possible. Children also need to be informed about what is going to happen, and they should have input in the decisions that are being made, if they are able to do so. Contrary to widely held belief, we do not protect children when we keep them in the dark. Children who have been abused have a right to be part of the decision-making process after their abuse.

Parents need to seek out the best and most experienced people in the field and be willing to go to higher levels if they are dissatisfied with the way they or their children are being treated. It cannot be assumed that everyone is adequately trained or able to be effective in every situation.

After a report is made, children are often interviewed repeatedly. As a parent, you have the right to question this process, to request that interviews be audiotaped, videotaped, and consolidated to prevent what professionals call "revictimization" of your child. If your child is to testify, be sure he or she understands what will happen,

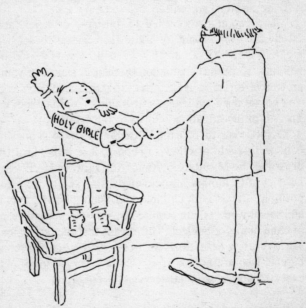

what kinds of questions will be asked, and what is expected. Finally, be sure your child understands that the perpetrator will be present.

While I believe that we must report, that we must find better ways to allow children to testify, that child abuse must be treated as a serious crime, the sad truth is: It is not. Sex abusers have the lowest conviction rate of any crime. DeVine reported in 1978 that only one in every sixty reported cases resulted in a conviction. Those convicted served an average of less than twelve months in jail.

This is changing. Treatment programs for abusers are expanding, innovative programs are requiring treatment rather than incarceration, public demand is resulting in stiffer sentences for repeat offenders, new and creative legislation is being passed that recognizes the special nature of crimes against children. It is not enough, but every case that is reported brings closer the day when sexual abuse of children will no longer be an ever-present possibility.

Is Therapy Necessary?

Parents often consider therapy unnecessary for child sexual abuse victims, particularly for boys. Parents say things to me like *"Let's let him forget it. He doesn't seem upset to me."* *Everything we know about child sexual abuse tells us that its effects are long-lasting and devastating.*

It is not true that children forget if the adults around them do not talk about it or allow them to talk about it. Sexual abuse incidents are intensely real for children, whether they talk about it or not.

One of the most important factors to a child's recovery is the placing of responsibility where it lies—with the perpetrator. Parents are often not able to adequately communicate this fact to children, and a professional can be very important to the child's ability to resolve the many issues that arise after sexual abuse.

The degree of impact sexual abuse has on a child is determined by several factors:

▶ **The type and severity of the abuse.**

▶ **The relationship of the perpetrator to the child.**

▶ **How long the abuse continued.**

▶ **The reaction of the people the child tells.**

▶ **Support available to the child to fully recover.**

There are professionals who know how to work with children who have been sexually abused. Therapists can help children to understand that what happened wasn't their fault and that they didn't do anything wrong. Through treatment, children can reestablish their sense of trust in adults and themselves. This may take two weeks or two years, depending on the child and the abuse. Whatever, it is remarkable to watch children recover from the subtle and profound effects of abuse. If your child is sexually abused, seek professional help.

CHAPTER 11
Being a Responsible Adult

As adults learn more about child abuse and abduction, they begin to evaluate their behavior toward others' children and even their own. They ask questions like "Am I being too affectionate?" One common feeling is to withdraw, to be less playful and affectionate with children, lest their actions be misinterpreted or misunderstood. While this is an understandable reaction, holding back is *not* an effective way to respond to this problem. It is enough to recognize the needs of children and to respond appropriately.

RULES FOR RESPONSIBLE STRANGERS

We know we are safe, harmless, and well-intentioned, and yet we look exactly the same to a child as an offender might look. It is important to be friendly, but we've got to balance that friendliness with a recognition of the realities for children.

As strangers, we too must follow the stranger rules. We need to avoid starting up casual conversations with children *who are not with an adult*. This means that we shouldn't ask children who are alone for directions, for the time, for assistance, or chat with them about their dog, a toy, or whatever.

While we know we represent no threat, those same comments or requests can be made by the "nicest people in the world" who later turn out to be dangerous. *Children obviously can't read minds, so they have no way of knowing whom they should talk to. They have to follow the stranger rules with all strangers, even you.*

Here are some situations where we should follow the rules:

▶ What if a child approaches you in the park and wants to talk? A parent is present, but not really watching. One option is to ask the child if Mom or Dad said it was okay to talk with you. If not, tell the child to get permission before talking to you because he or she doesn't know you.

▶ What if you are giving samples or treats away as a part of your job or at a school event? Always ask parents if it's all right to give the item to their children before giving it to them. This reinforces the parents' role as protector when they are with their children.

▶ What if you need to drop something off for a business associate whose children you do not know? Don't ask the children to take the item. Instead, deliver it directly to the parent.

With older children, it is generally all right to make small talk in a public setting when other people are around. It is not as appropriate in a more isolated setting. You should allow children to take the lead in terms of what *they* are comfortable with. Be sensitive to small signs that indicate children are uncomfortable, and stop talking.

I know that this seems restrictive and creates some uncertainty about how we should behave with children. As often as I speak about this, I still have to monitor myself to follow the rules with children I don't know. But when I see children who follow the rules for strangers with me, I know they are less vulnerable to the "friendly" stranger who might hurt them.

Lost Children

On the other hand, children sometimes need help. When they do, again because *you* know you are "safe," it is essential that you stop and help. In doing so, be consistent with what we've said about strangers.

When children are lost, approach them, ask if they are lost, and escort them to the front of the store where a clerk or manager can page their parents. If at all possible, do not leave them until they are reunited with their parents. It is not appropriate to take them to get a soda or to wander around the store looking for their parents.

Helping lost children is an excellent opportunity to teach them what they should do the next time they're in a similar situation. Children are very receptive when they're lost, as are their parents, to hearing about strategies that you've found work with your own children.

Children We Know

The suggestions for teaching prevention of sexual abuse to your own children can be applied to other children. For example, when you are greeted with a big hug from the child of a friend, it feels terrific. But if the child pulls away even though you'd like another hug, the best response is "That was a nice hug. Thank you for letting me know you were ready to get down."

Another example. If you're stroking your nephew's hair and he asks you to stop or wiggles away, you can say, "I didn't know you don't like that. Thanks for telling me to stop. If I forget, you can remind me."

What if the child of a friend is consistently shy and her father keeps encouraging her to talk and be affectionate with you because you're a friend? You might say, "I'm really *your* friend right now, not hers. She'll get to know me as time goes along and then she can decide if we want to be friends. For right now, it's okay for her to be just the way she is, so let's not push her."

Children show us more often than they tell us what they like and don't like. We can give them permission to speak up and let them know that we don't feel rejected just because they ask us not to do something. Experiencing this with a variety of adults greatly strengthens their ability to use the prevention techniques when they need to.

CHILD ADVOCACY

In teaching prevention, we ask children to tell us what is happening to them as a way of helping us to help them. Do we listen? What if a child whispers to us, "This man won't let me see my mommy." What do we say? How do we start? Do we dismiss it as the active imagination of a playful child? Even if we say something, the adult may respond with "Oh, she's always saying things like that to get attention." Do we walk away? Do we report it? Do we tag along to get the license number of their car?

If we see a screaming child being carried from a store, what do we think? What do we do? Most of us see a child having a temper tantrum. (Children, by the way, see this as a child in trouble with no one helping, not even Mom and Dad.) Are we able to ask what's happening to that child? One option would be to approach and say, "Are you giving your mother a hard time?" If the child responds with "This is not my mother, she's taking me away." the situation has changed dramatically.

How often do we remain silent, wishing not to interfere, afraid we will falsely accuse someone *or* of the possible consequences of our intrusion? It takes courage to speak up forthrightly but each of us must do what we can do to support children, to report what's being done to them. The law protects individuals who report suspected child abuse and neglect. You have the right to remain anonymous and you cannot be sued or found liable for damages unless it can be proven that you were malicious and deliberate in filing a false report.

We are teaching children to take care of themselves when they're by themselves. At the same time, children need our care too. If each of us can become an advocate for each of the children in our life, those we know and those we don't, the abuse of children would significantly diminish. This is not simple or easy. It is, however, a process, a beginning, by which we can reduce the isolation and victimization of children.

When we speak up for children they learn to speak up for themselves. That is the challenge.

Appendix

For More Information

For more information on school and community programs for the prevention of sexual abuse and abduction, please write:

Sherryll Kerns Kraizer
Health Education Systems
P.O. Box 1235
New York, New York 10116

Acknowledgments

Several women have helped shape the direction of prevention of sexual abuse over the last five years. Collectively they have made a positive difference in the lives of hundreds of thousands of children. I wish to acknowledge the dedication, work, and insights of:

Caren Adams
Cordelia Anderson
Flora Colao
Mary Dietzel
Ann Downer
Jennifer Fay

Ruth Harms
Tamar Hosansky
Donna James
Linda Tschirhart Sanford
Jo Stowell
Oralee Wachter

Annotated Bibliography

The following books are all highly recommended. Most must be special ordered.

Books for Children

Burns, Marilyn. *I Am Not a Short Adult: Getting Good at Being a Kid.* Boston: Little, Brown and Co., 1977. Paperback, $5.95.
Exceptional discussion of communication, rules, feelings, money, having fun, working hard, rights, responsibilities, and assertiveness. Ages 8–12.

Chaback, Elaine, and Fortunato, Pat. *The Official Kids Survival Kit: How to Do Things on Your Own.* Boston: Little, Brown and Co., 1981. Paperback, $9.95.
Invaluable resource. Encyclopedia-style reference for handling such varied situations as boredom, loneliness, jealousy, baby-sitting, going to camp, fixing breakfast, working parents, and various aspects of staying alone. Ages 8–12.

Le Shan, Eda. *What Makes Me Feel This Way?: Growing Up with Human Emotions.* New York: Macmillan Books, 1972. Paperback, $9.95.
Straightforward, honest, and understanding discussion of the range of feelings children have and how confusing they can be. Very supportive of individual differences. Ages 6–12.

Palmer, Pat. *Liking Myself.* San Luis Obispo, CA: Impact Publishers, 1983. Paperback, $4.50.
Introduction to feelings, self-esteem, and assertiveness. Reinforces listening to your feelings, your inner voice, and speaking up for yourself. Ages 4–7.

Palmer, Pat. *The Mouse, the Monster and Me.* San Luis Obispo, CA: Impact Publishers, 1982. Paperback, $4.50.
Strong reinforcement of saying no, dealing with hurtful and confusing situations, rights and responsibilities, and communication skills. Especially beneficial for children who tend to be shy or aggressive. Ages 7–11.

Stowell, Jo, and Dietzel, Mary. *My Very Own Book About Me.* Spokane, WA: Lutheran Social Services of Washington, 1982. Paperback, $4.50.
Teaches prevention of sexual abuse without fear or embarrassment. Teaches positive self-concept, self-esteem, and self-assurance. Especially useful for teaching prevention after children have experienced abuse. Ages 4–10.

Wachter, Oralee. *No More Secrets for Me.* Boston: Little, Brown and Co., 1983. Paperback, $4.95.
Positive and discreet stories about preventing sexual abuse. Reinforces teaching children to speak up, to say no, and to tell when someone violates their trust. Ages 6–12.

Books for Parents

Alberti, Robert E., and Emmons, Michael L. *Your Perfect Right: A Guide to Assertive Behavior*. San Luis Obispo, CA: Impact Publishers, 1978. Paperback, $6.95.
The best straightforward outline available for basic assertiveness training. Directed at adults, but the principles are easily adapted for children.

Auerbach, Steveanne. *The Whole Child Sourcebook*. New York: Perigee Books, 1981. Paperback, $8.95.
Step-by-step sourcebook for parenting from pregnancy to age twelve. Includes information on resources, organizations, and books.

Bartz, Wayne R. *Surviving with Kids: A Lifeline for Overwhelmed Parents*. San Luis Obispo, CA: Impact Publishers, 1978. Paperback, $4.95.
Practical aid for parents of preteens, but the ideas are applicable to all ages.

Dinkmeyer, Don, and McKay, Gary D. *STEP: Systematic Training for Effective Parenting*. Circle Pines, MN: American Guidance Service, 1976. Paperback, $6.95.
Basic principles and methods of childrearing. For parents and professionals.

Faber, Adele, and Mazlish, Elaine. *How to Talk So Kids Will Listen and Listen So Kids Will Talk*. New York: Avon Books, 1982. Paperback, $4.95.
Well-organized and readable book about communicating. Techniques are clearly presented from the parents' and child's point of view.

Mitchell, Grace. *The Day Care Book*. New York: Fawcett Columbine, 1979. Paperback, $4.95.
A must for any parent considering day care. Mitchell addresses fully the developmental needs of children and how to find a day-care arrangement that meets them.

Morris, Michelle. *If I Should Die Before I Wake*. Boston: Houghton Mifflin, 1982. Hardcover, $12.95.
Intensely realistic fictionalization of father/daughter incest told through the eyes of the daughter.

Pogrebin, Letty Cottin. *Growing Up Free: Raising Your Child in the 80's*. New York: Bantam Books, 1980. Paperback, $8.95.
The original blueprint for helping children to reach their full potential, free of sex-role stereotypes.

REFERENCES

Chapter 1

Page 11:
According to the National Center for Missing and Exploited Children, up to 50,000 children disappear each year and their cases remain unsolved.

National Center for Missing and Exploited Children, Washington, D.C., 1984.

Page 11:
The Kinsey report in 1953 found that one in every four women had been sexually abused as a child.

Kinsey, A; Pomeroy, W.; Marin, C.; and Gebhard, P. *Sexual Behavior in the Human Female*. Philadelphia: Saunders, 1953.

Page 11:
Researcher Diana Russell in 1981 reported 38% of the women participating in her study had experienced sexual abuse by age 18.

Russell, Diana E.H. "The Incidence and Prevalence of Intrafamilial and Extrafamilial Sexual Abuse of Female Children" *Child Abuse and Neglect*, 7:137. 1983.

Page 12:
The Child Sexual Abuse Prevention Project reported from 30-46% of all children are sexually assaulted in some way by age 18.

Kent, Cordelia A. *Child Sexual Abuse Prevention Project*, Hennepin County Attorney's Office, Minneapolis, MN pg 2. 1979.

Page 12:
Cases involving boys are less often reported, but recent research indicates they may be at equal risk.

Kent, Cordelia A. *Child Sexual Abuse Prevention Project*, p. 17.

Finkelhor, David. *Sexually Victimized Children*. The Free Press, New York, 1979. p. 138.

Page 12:
Experts agree that 85-90% of all incidents of sexual abuse take place with someone the child knows and trusts, not a stranger.

Adams, Caren and Fay, Jennifer. *No More Secrets*. Impact Publishers, San Luis Obispo, CA, 1981. p. 8.

DeFrancis, Vincent. *Protecting the Child Victim of Sex Crimes Committed by Adults*. Denver, CO.: American Humane Association, 1969.

Russell, Diana E.H. "Incidence and Prevalence of Sexual Abuse of Female Children", p. 144.

Page 12:
David Finkelhor's research in 1979 reported that 26% of the students in his survey were sexually abused by a relative.

Finkelhor, David. *Sexually Victimized Children*. p. 86.

Page 12:
The Children's Defense Fund estimates that 5.2 million children 13 and under are left without adult supervision each day.
The Child Case Handbook. Children's Defense Fund. Washington, D.C., 1982.

Chapter 3

Page 38:
While most pedophiles are men, his [Finkelhor] research indicates that at least ten percent of all perpetrators are women.
Finkelhor, David. *Sexually Victimized Children*. pp. 78-80.

Page 38:
Gene Abel and Judith Becker report that the average molester of girl children will molest 62 victims and the average molester of boy children will molest 30 victims.
Sanford, Linda T. *The Silent Children*. Anchor Press/Doubleday, New York, 1980. p. 85.

Page 39:
. . . Diana Russell, in one of the most comprehensive studies to date found that 16% of the women participating in her study had experienced sexual abuse with a family member at least five years older. Father/daughter incest was reported by 4.5% of the women.
Russell, Diana E.H. "Incidence and Prevalence of Sexual Abuse of Female Children", p. 38.

Page 39:
Children are at greater risk for abuse with boyfriends and new stepfathers.
Finkelhor, David. *Sexually Victimized Children*, p. 122.
Russell, Diana E.H. "Incidence and Prevalence of Sexual Abuse of Female Children", p. 140.

Chapter 10

Page 116:
DeVine reported in 1978 that only one in every sixty reported cases resulted in conviction. Those convicted served an average of less than twelve months in jail.
DeVine, R. "Some Violence Statistics" *American Psychological Association Monitor*, February, 1978.

ABOUT THE AUTHOR

Sherryll Kerns Kraizer is an educator, consultant, and one of the country's foremost experts in personal safety training for children. She has her Master's degree in Special Education and Psychology from the University of Kansas.

Because of her work with children who had been victims of sexual abuse and abduction, Ms. Kraizer created the *Children Need to Know* program which teaches personal safety directly to small groups of children and their parents. It has been presented to over 50,000 children and their parents and was featured in the Emmy Award–winning television production, *Saying No To Strangers*.

Ms. Kraizer is director of Health Education Systems, Inc., and continues to develop programs which meet the changing needs of children and families. She lives north of New York City with her husband, Al Kraizer.